M000224021

Whatever you eat or drink
or whatever you do,
you must do all
for the glory of God.

—

1 Corinthians 10:31 NLT

Freeman-Smith, a division of Worthy Media, Inc.

134 Franklin Road, Suite 200, Brentwood, Tennessee 37027

The quoted ideas expressed in this book (but not Scripture verses) are not, in all cases, exact quotations, as some have been edited for clarity and brevity. In all cases, the author has attempted to maintain the speaker's original intent. In some cases, quoted material for this book was obtained from secondary sources, primarily print media. While every effort was made to ensure the accuracy of these sources, the accuracy cannot be guaranteed. For additions, deletions, corrections, or clarifications in future editions of this text, please write Freeman-Smith.

The Holy Bible, King James Version

The Holy Bible, New King James Version (NKJV) Copyright © 1982 by Thomas Nelson, Inc. Used by permission.

New Century Version®. (NCV) Copyright © 1987, 1988, 1991 by Word Publishing, a division of Thomas Nelson, Inc. All rights reserved. Used by permission.

International Children's Bible®, New Century Version®. (ICB) Copyright © 1986, 1988, 1999 by Tommy Nelson™, a division of Thomas Nelson, Inc. All rights reserved. Used by permission.

The Holman Christian Standard Bible™ (HCSB) Copyright © 1999, 2000, 2001 by Holman Bible Publishers. Used by permission.

The Holy Bible, New International Version®. (NIV) Copyright © 1973, 1978, 1984 International Bible Society. Used by permission of Zondervan. All rights reserved.

The Holy Bible. New Living Translation (NLT) copyright © 1996 Tyndale Charitable Trust. Used by permission of Tyndale House Publishers.

The New American Standard Bible®, (NASB) Copyright © 1960, 1962, 1963, 1968, 1971, 1972, 1973, 1975, 1977, 1995 by The Lockman Foundation. Used by permission.

Scripture taken from The Message. (MSG) Copyright © 1993, 1994, 1995, 1996, 2000, 2001, 2002. Used by permission of NavPress Publishing Group.

Cover Design by Kim Russell / Wahoo Designs
Page Layout by Bart Dawson

ISBN 978-1-60587-436-4
ISBN 978-1-60587-498-2 (Special Edition)

Printed in the United States of America

1 2 3 4 5—CHG—16 15 14 13 12

God's Guide
to FOOD,
FITNESS,
and FAITH,
for Women

30 Biblical Principles for Better Health

TABLE OF CONTENTS

A Message to Readers   *30 days*   7
                    1/26/13

Introduction   9

1. God's Plan for Better Health   11

2. Your Partnership with God   20

3. Don't Go on a Diet, Change Your Lifestyle   29

4. If Not Now, When?   38

5. Respecting Your Body   46

6. The Right Kind of Exercise for You   54

7. Protecting Your Emotional Health   62

8. It Takes Discipline   72

9. Healthy Priorities   81

10. Your Choices Matter   90

11. Beyond the Setbacks   98

12. So Many Temptations   103

13. Your Body, Your Choices   108

14. Entrusting Your Hopes to God   116

15. The Power of Optimism   121

16. Asking for God's Help   126

17. Spiritual Health, Spiritual Growth   135

18. Perspective and Balance   143

19. Recharging Your Spiritual Batteries   152

20. Making God's Priorities Your Priorities   160

21. Lifetime Learning   165

22. God's Plan for Your Health   170

23. Getting Enough Rest?   178

24. Misdirected Worship: The Tragedy of
Addiction   188

25. Be Patient and Trust God   198

26. The Power of Daily Worship and
Meditation   203

27. Putting Faith Above Feelings   212

28. You're Accountable   217

29. Fitness Is a Form of Worship   222

30. Your Physical and Spiritual Fitness:
Who's in Charge?   232

A MESSAGE TO READERS

A wise man will hear and increase learning,
and a man of understanding will attain wise counsel.

—

Proverbs 1:5 NKJV

The advice in this book is general in nature, and your circumstances are specific to you. For that reason, we strongly suggest that you consult your physician before beginning any new regimen of physical exercise or diet. Don't depend upon this book—or any other book like it—to be your sole source of information on matters pertaining to your health. Instead, consider Proverbs 1:5 and seek wise counsel from a variety of sources, especially your personal physician, before making major health-related decisions.

INTRODUCTION

Countless books have been written on the topics of health and fitness. But if you're a Christian, you probably already own at least one copy—and more likely several copies—of the world's foremost guide to spiritual, physical, and emotional fitness. That book is the Holy Bible. The Bible is the irreplaceable guidebook for faithful believers—like you—who seek God's wisdom and His truth.

God has a plan for every aspect of your life, including your food, your fitness, and your faith. But God will not force His plans upon you; to the contrary, He has given you the ability to make choices. The consequences of those choices help determine the quality and the tone of your life. This little book is intended to help you make wise choices—choices that will lead to spiritual, physical, and emotional health—by encouraging you to rely heavily upon the promises of God's Holy Word.

Health is a gift from God. What we do with that gift is determined, to a surprising extent, by the person we see every time we gaze into the mirror. If we squander our health—or if we take it for granted—we do a profound disservice to ourselves and to our loved ones. But God has other plans. He commands us to treat our bodies, our minds, and our souls with the utmost care. And that's exactly what we should do.

If you seek to protect and to enhance your spiritual, emotional, and physical health, these pages will help, but they offer no shortcuts. Healthy living is a journey, not a destination, and that journey requires discipline. If you're willing to make the step-by-step journey toward improved health, rest assured that God is taking careful note of your progress . . . and He's quietly urging you to take the next step.

GOD'S PLAN FOR BETTER HEALTH

A prudent person foresees the danger ahead
and takes precautions.
The simpleton goes blindly on
and suffers the consequences.

—

Proverbs 27:12 NLT

THE BIBLICAL PRINCIPLE

When you form a deeper relationship with God,
you can start establishing healthier habits,
beginning now.

This book contains 30 chapters, each of which addresses an important Biblical truth about your fitness, your faith, or your future. If you read each chapter carefully—and if you implement the ideas that you find there—these principles will have a profound impact on your own life and upon the lives of your loved ones.

If you're like most women, you've already tried, perhaps on many occasions, to form healthier habits. You've employed your own willpower in a noble effort to create a new, improved, healthier you. You've probably tried to improve various aspects of your spiritual, physical, or emotional health. Perhaps you've gone on diets, or made New Year's resolutions, or tried the latest self-help fad in an attempt to finally make important changes in your life. And if you're like most women, you've been successful, for a while. But eventually, those old familiar habits came creeping back into your life, and the improvements that you had made proved to be temporary. This book is intended to help you build a series of healthy habits for your Christian walk . . . and then make those habits stick.

As you read through this text, you'll be asked to focus on three major areas of your life: diet, fitness, and faith. You will be asked to depend less upon your own willpower and more upon God's power. And, you will be asked to weave timeless Biblical principles into the fabric of your everyday life. When you do these things, you will form a working relationship with the Creator. And, there's absolutely no limit to the things that the two of you, working together, can do.

FOOD FOR THOUGHT
VERY BIG PORTIONS
MAKE VERY LITTLE SENSE

Do you dine out often? If so, be careful. Most restaurants stay in business by serving big portions of tasty food. Unfortunately, most restaurant food is high in calories, sugar, and fat. You will probably eat healthier meals if you prepare those meals at home instead of eating out.

MORE FROM GOD'S WORD

Dear friend, I pray that you may prosper in every way and be in good health, just as your soul prospers.

3 John 1:2 HCSB

Do you not know that your body is a sanctuary of the Holy Spirit who is in you, whom you have from God? You are not your own, for you were bought at a price; therefore glorify God in your body.

1 Corinthians 6:19-20 HCSB

Guard your heart above all else, for it is the source of life.

Proverbs 4:23 HCSB

Acquire wisdom—how much better it is than gold! And acquire understanding—it is preferable to silver.

Proverbs 16:16 HCSB

Therefore, everyone who hears these words of Mine and acts on them will be like a sensible man who built his house on the rock. The rain fell, the rivers rose, and the winds blew and pounded that house. Yet it didn't collapse, because its foundation was on the rock.

Matthew 7:24–25 HCSB

MORE THOUGHTS ABOUT
YOUR HABITS

You can build up a set of good habits so that you habitually take the Christian way without thought.

E. Stanley Jones

You will never change your life until you change something you do daily.

John Maxwell

He who does not overcome small faults, shall fall little by little into greater ones.

Thomas à Kempis

Begin to be now what you will be hereafter.

St. Jerome

Habit is a cable; we weave a thread of it each day, and at last we cannot break it.

Thomas Mann

15

FORMING HEALTHY HABITS

I t's an old saying and a true one: First, you make your habits, and then your habits make you. Some habits will inevitably bring you closer to God; other habits will lead you away from the path He has chosen for you. If you sincerely desire to improve your spiritual health, you must honestly examine the habits that make up the fabric of your day. And you must abandon those habits that are displeasing to God.

If you trust God, and if you keep asking for His help, He can transform your life. If you sincerely ask Him to help you, the same God who created the universe will help you defeat the harmful habits that have heretofore defeated you. So, if at first you don't succeed, keep praying. God is listening, and He's ready to help you become a better person if you ask Him . . . so ask today.

WORKING IT OUT
TALK TO YOUR DOCTOR ABOUT EXERCISE

Before you begin a major new exercise program, see your doctor: As the old saying goes, it's better to be safe than sorry.

MOVING MOUNTAINS

Every life—including yours—is a series of successes and failures, celebrations and disappointments, joys and sorrows. Every step of the way, through every triumph and tragedy, God will stand by your side and strengthen you . . . if you have faith in Him. Jesus taught His disciples that if they had faith, they could move mountains. You can too.

When a suffering woman sought healing by merely touching the hem of His cloak, Jesus replied, "Daughter, be of good comfort; thy faith hath made thee whole" (Matthew 9:22 KJV). The message to believers of every generation is clear: we must live by faith every day.

When you place your faith, your trust, indeed your life in the hands of Christ Jesus, you'll be amazed at the marvelous things He can do with you and through you. So strengthen your faith through praise, through worship, through Bible study, and through prayer. And trust God's plans. With Him, all things are possible, and He stands ready to open a world of possibilities to you . . . if you have faith.

MORE FROM GOD'S WORD ABOUT FAITH

If you do not stand firm in your faith, then you will not stand at all.

Isaiah 7:9 HCSB

Be alert, stand firm in the faith, be brave and strong.

1 Corinthians 16:13 HCSB

For we walk by faith, not by sight.

2 Corinthians 5:7 HCSB

Now faith is the reality of what is hoped for, the proof of what is not seen.

Hebrews 11:1 HCSB

STRENGTHENING YOUR FAITH
INTEGRATING GOD'S WORD INTO YOUR LIFE

Perhaps you have tended to divide the concerns of your life into two categories: "spiritual" and "other." If so, it's time to reconsider. God intends you to integrate His commandments into every aspect of your life, and that includes your physical and emotional health, too.

NOTES TO YOURSELF

In the space below, make notes about the healthy habits that you'd like to establish—and the unhealthy habits you'd like to change—during the next 30 days.

eat less ; move more
be calm without eating

YOUR PARTNERSHIP WITH GOD

So now we can rejoice in our wonderful new relationship with God—all because of what our Lord Jesus Christ has done for us in making us friends of God.

—

Romans 5:11 NLT

THE BIBLICAL PRINCIPLE

Your journey toward improved health can be,
and should be,
a journey that you make with God.

Physical fitness, like every other aspect of your life, begins and ends with God. If you'd like to adopt a healthier lifestyle, God is willing to help. In fact, if you sincerely wish to create a healthier you—either physically, emotionally or spiritually—God is anxious to be your silent partner in that endeavor, but it's up to you to ask for His help.

The journey toward improved health is not only a common-sense exercise in personal discipline, it is also a spiritual journey ordained by our Creator. God does not intend that we abuse our bodies by giving in to excessive appetites or to slothful behavior. To the contrary, God has instructed us to protect our physical bodies to the greatest extent we can. To do otherwise is to disobey Him.

God has a plan for every facet of your life, and His plan includes provisions for your spiritual, physical, and emotional health. But, He expects you to do your fair share of the work! In a world that is chock-full of tasty temptations, you may find it all too easy to make unhealthy choices. Your challenge, of course, is to resist those unhealthy choices by every means you can, including prayer. And you can be sure that whenever you ask for God's help, He will give it.

Our world is teeming with temptations and distractions that can rob you of the physical, emotional, and spiritual fitness that might otherwise be yours. And if you're not careful, the struggles and stresses of everyday living can rob you of the peace that should rightfully be yours because of your personal relationship with Christ. So take time each day to have a personal training session with your Savior. Don't be a woman who's satisfied with occasional visits to church on Sunday morning; build a relationship with Jesus that deepens day by day. When you do, you will most certainly encounter the subtle hand of the Father. Then, if you are wise, you will take His hand and follow God as He leads you on the path to a healthier, happier life.

FOOD FOR THOUGHT
START SLOWLY AND USE COMMON SENSE

Adopt healthy habits you can stick with. In other words, don't starve yourself. And if you're beginning an exercise regimen, start slowly. Be moderate, even in your moderation.

MORE FROM GOD'S WORD

Don't you know that you are God's sanctuary and that the Spirit of God lives in you?

1 Corinthians 3:16 HCSB

Now the God of all grace, who called you to His eternal glory in Christ Jesus, will personally restore, establish, strengthen, and support you.

1 Peter 5:10 HCSB

Peace, peace to you, and peace to your helpers! For your God helps you.

1 Chronicles 12:18 NKJV

The LORD is my strength and song, and He has become my salvation; He is my God, and I will praise Him.

Exodus 15:2 NKJV

For I am persuaded that neither death nor life, nor angels nor rulers, nor things present, nor things to come, nor powers, nor height, nor depth, nor any other created thing will have the power to separate us from the love of God that is in Christ Jesus our Lord!

Romans 8:38-39 HCSB

MORE THOUGHTS ABOUT
GOD'S SUPPORT

Measure the size of the obstacles against the size of God.

Beth Moore

God uses our most stumbling, faltering faith-steps as the open door to His doing for us "more than we ask or think."

Catherine Marshall

God wants to reveal Himself as your heavenly Father. When you wonder which way to turn, you can grasp His strong hand, and He'll guide you along life's path.

Lisa Whelchel

If you desire to improve your physical well-being and your emotional outlook, increasing your faith can help you.

John Maxwell

God will never lead you where His strength cannot keep you.

Barbara Johnson

SAY NO TO UNHEALTHY FOODS

Eating unhealthy foods is habit-forming. And if you have acquired the unfortunate habit of eating unhealthy foods, then God wants you to start making changes today.

Take a few minutes to think about your eating habits. Do you gobble down snack foods while watching television? If so, stop. Do you drink high-calorie soft drinks or feast on unhealthy snacks like potato chips or candy? If so, you're doing yourself a disservice. Do you delight in high-fat, high-calorie foods that taste good for a few seconds but accumulate on your waistline for years? Do you load up your plate until food falls off the edge? And then do you feel obligated to eat every last bite? If so, it's time to think long and hard about the serious consequences of indulging in such unhealthy habits.

Poor eating habits are easy to make and hard to break, but break them you must. Otherwise, you'll be disobeying God's commandments while causing yourself great harm.

Maintaining a healthy lifestyle is a journey, not a destination, and that journey requires discipline. But rest assured that if you and your loved ones are willing to make the step-by-step journey toward a healthier diet, God is taking careful note of your progress . . . and He's quietly urging you to take the next step.

GOD'S PROTECTION

I n a world filled with dangers and temptations, God is the ultimate armor. In a world filled with misleading messages, God's Word is the ultimate truth. In a world filled with more frustrations than we can count, God's Son offers the ultimate peace. Will you accept God's peace and wear God's armor against the dangers of our world?

Sometimes, in the crush of everyday life, God may seem far away, but He is not. God is everywhere you have ever been and everywhere you will ever go. He is with you night and day; He knows your thoughts and your prayers. He is your ultimate Protector. And, when you earnestly seek His protection, you will find it because He is here—always—waiting patiently for you to reach out to Him.

WORKING IT OUT
IT'S UP TO YOU

The benefits of exercise are both physical and emotional. But no one can exercise for you; it's up to you to exercise, or not.

MORE FROM GOD'S WORD ABOUT GOD'S LOVE

For God loved the world in this way: He gave His only Son, so that everyone who believes in Him will not perish but have eternal life.

John 3:16 HCSB

For the Lord is good, and His love is eternal; His faithfulness endures through all generations.

Psalm 100:5 HCSB

Draw near to God, and He will draw near to you.

James 4:8 HCSB

STRENGTHENING YOUR FAITH
IT'S THE BEST-SELLING BOOK OF ALL TIME FOR A REASON

Ruth Bell Graham, wife of evangelist Billy Graham, observed: "The Reference Point for the Christian is the Bible. All values, judgments, and attitudes must be gauged in relationship to this Reference Point." Make certain that you're an avid reader of God's best-seller, and make sure that you keep reading it as long as you live!

NOTES TO YOURSELF

In the space below, make notes about the times in your life when God has protected you and led you out of danger. Then, prayerfully ask God to help you make the spiritual and physical journey to improved health.

_____

_____

_____

_____

_____

_____

_____

_____

_____

_____

_____

_____

_____

_____

DON'T GO ON A DIET, CHANGE YOUR LIFESTYLE

Their end is destruction;
their god is their stomach;
their glory is in their shame.
They are focused on earthly things.

—

Philippians 3:19 HCSB

THE BIBLICAL PRINCIPLE

It takes wisdom to be moderate;
moderation is wisdom in action.

If you want to lose weight, don't you dare go on a diet! It's a sad fact, but true: in the vast majority of cases, diets simply don't work. In fact, one study that examined the results of popular diets conducted that nearly 100% of dieters suffered almost "complete relapse after 3 to 5 years." In other words, dieters almost always return to their pre-diet weights (or, in many cases, to even higher weight levels).

If diets don't work, what should you do if you weigh more than you should? The answer is straightforward: If you need to lose weight, don't start dieting; change your lifestyle.

Your current weight is the result of the number of calories that you have taken into your body versus the number of calories that you have burned. If you seek to lower your weight, then you must burn more calories (by engaging in more vigorous physical activities), or take in fewer calories (by eating more sensibly), or both. It's as simple as that.

Many of us are remarkably ill informed and amazingly apathetic about the foods we eat. We feast on high-fat fast foods. We swoon over sweets. We order up—and promptly pack away—prodigious portions. The result is a society in which too many of us become the human equivalents of the portions we purchase: oversized.

A healthier strategy, of course, is to pay more attention to the nutritional properties of our foods and less attention their taste. But for those of us who have become accustomed to large quantities of full-flavored, high-calorie foods, old memories indeed die hard.

Should we count every calorie that we ingest from now until the day the Good Lord calls us home? Probably not. When we focus too intently upon weight reduction, we may make weight loss even harder to achieve. Instead, we should eliminate from our diets the foods that are obviously bad for us and we should eat more of the foods that are obviously good for us. And of course, we should eat sensible amounts, not prodigious portions.

How hard is it for us to know the nutritional properties of the foods we eat? Not very hard. In the grocery store, almost every food item is clearly marked. In fast-food restaurants, the fat and calorie contents are posted on the wall (although the print is incredibly small, and with good reason: the health properties of these tasty tidbits are, in most cases, so poor that we should rename them "fat foods").

As informed adults, we have access to all the information that we need to make healthy dietary choices. Now it's up to each of us to make wise dietary choices, or not. Those choices are ours, and so are their consequences.

MORE FROM GOD'S WORD

Do not carouse with drunkards and gluttons, for they are on their way to poverty.

Proverbs 23:20-21 NLT

Do you like honey? Don't eat too much of it, or it will make you sick!

Proverbs 25:16 NLT

Be sober! Be on the alert! Your adversary the Devil is prowling around like a roaring lion, looking for anyone he can devour.

1 Peter 5:8 HCSB

FOOD FOR THOUGHT
DON'T SKIP MEALS

Are you skipping meals? Don't do it. Skipping meals isn't healthy, and it isn't a sensible way to lose weight, either.

MORE THOUGHTS ABOUT
MODERATION

It's not that some people have willpower and some don't. It's that some people are ready to change and others are not.

James Gordon, M.D.

You can look at your calorie count in the same way you might look at a bank account. Every mouthful of food is a deposit and every activity that requires energy is a withdrawal. If we deposit more than we withdraw, our surplus grows larger and larger.

John Maxwell

We are all created differently. We share a common need to balance the different parts of our lives.

Dr. Walt Larimore

To many, total abstinence is easier than perfect moderation.

St. Augustine

Failure is the path of least persistence.

Anonymous

MODERATION LEADS TO ABUNDANCE

If you're a woman who sincerely seeks the abundant life that Christ has promised, you must learn to control your appetites before they control you. Good habits, like bad ones, are habit-forming. The sooner you acquire the habit of moderation, the better your chances for a long, happy, abundant life.

Are you running short on willpower? If so, perhaps you haven't yet asked God to give you strength. The Bible promises that God offers His power to those righteous men and women who earnestly seek it. If your willpower has failed you on numerous occasions, then it's time to turn your weaknesses over to God. If you've been having trouble standing on your own two feet, perhaps it's time to drop to your knees in prayer.

WORKING IT OUT
ALL HANDS ON DECK

If you're trying to reshape your physique or your life, don't try to do it alone. Ask for the support and encouragement of your family members and friends. You'll improve your odds of success if you enlist your own cheering section.

MODERATION IS WISDOM IN ACTION

Moderation and wisdom are traveling companions. If we are wise, we must learn to temper our appetites, our desires, and our impulses. When we do, we are blessed, in part, because God has created a world in which temperance is rewarded and intemperance is inevitably punished.

When we allow our appetites to run wild, they usually do. When we abandon moderation, we forfeit the inner peace that God offers—but does not guarantee—to His children. When we live intemperate lives, we rob ourselves of countless blessings that would have otherwise been ours.

God's instructions are clear: if we seek to live wisely, we must be moderate in our appetites and disciplined in our behavior. To do otherwise is an affront to Him . . . and to ourselves.

STRENGTHENING YOUR FAITH
NEVER STOP STUDYING GOD'S WORD

Even if you've been studying the Bible for many years, you've still got lots to learn. Bible study should be a lifelong endeavor; make it your lifelong endeavor.

MORE FROM GOD'S WORD ABOUT
WISDOM

Therefore, everyone who hears these words of Mine and acts on them will be like a sensible man who built his house on the rock. The rain fell, the rivers rose, and the winds blew and pounded that house. Yet it didn't collapse, because its foundation was on the rock.

Matthew 7:24–25 HCSB

But from Him you are in Christ Jesus, who for us became wisdom from God, as well as righteousness, sanctification, and redemption.

1 Corinthians 1:30 HCSB

Now if any of you lacks wisdom, he should ask God, who gives to all generously and without criticizing, and it will be given to him.

James 1:5 HCSB

But the wisdom from above is first pure, then peace-loving, gentle, compliant, full of mercy and good fruits, without favoritism and hypocrisy.

James 3:17 HCSB

NOTES TO YOURSELF

In the space below, make notes about aspects of your life that will be improved when you eat more moderately and exercise more regularly.

IF NOT NOW, WHEN?

Therefore, get your minds ready for action,
being self-disciplined, and set your hope completely
on the grace to be brought to you
at the revelation of Jesus Christ.

—

1 Peter 1:13 HCSB

THE BIBLICAL PRINCIPLE

When it comes to food, fitness, or faith,
the best moment to begin major improvements
is the present moment.

I f you're determined to improve the state of your physical, spiritual, or emotional health, the best time to begin is now. But if you're like most people, you'll be tempted to put things off until tomorrow, or the next day, or the next.

The habit of putting things off until the last minute, along with its first cousin, the habit of making excuses for work that was never done, can be detrimental to your life, to your character, and to your health. Are you in the habit of doing what needs to be done when it needs to be done, or are you a dues-paying member of the Procrastinator's Club? If you're a woman who has already acquired the habit of doing things sooner rather than later, congratulations! But, if you find yourself putting off all those unpleasant tasks until later (or never), it's time to think about the consequences of your behavior.

One way that you can learn to defeat procrastination is by paying less attention to the sacrifices you're making today and more attention to the rewards you'll receive tomorrow. So, if you're trying to improve your fitness, or any other aspect of your life, don't spend endless hours fretting over your fate. Simply seek God's counsel and get busy. When you do, you will be richly rewarded because of your willingness to act.

MORE FROM GOD'S WORD

But be doers of the word and not hearers only.

James 1:22 HCSB

When you make a vow to God, don't delay fulfilling it, because He does not delight in fools. Fulfill what you vow.

Ecclesiastes 5:4 HCSB

For the hearers of the law are not righteous before God, but the doers of the law will be declared righteous.

Romans 2:13 HCSB

FOOD FOR THOUGHT
NOW IS THE TIME

Life is a gift—health must be earned. We earn good health by cultivating healthy habits. This is the right time for you to commit yourself to a more sensible lifestyle. So take a close look at your habits: how you eat, how you exercise, and how you think about your health. The only way that you'll revolutionize your physical health is to revolutionize the habits that make up the fabric of your day.

MORE THOUGHTS ABOUT
THE NEED TO TAKE ACTION NOW

We spend our lives dreaming of the future, not realizing that a little of it slips away every day.

Barbara Johnson

To learn new habits is everything, for it is to reach the substance of life. Life is a tissue of habits.

Henri Frédéric Amiel

Do noble things, do not dream them all day long.

Charles Kingsley

Never fail to do something because you don't feel like it. Sometimes you just have to do it now, and you'll feel like it later.

Marie T. Freeman

Measure the size of the obstacles against the size of God.

Beth Moore

HOW MANY CALORIES?

Of a thousand American adults who were surveyed in a recent poll, eighty-eight percent were unable to accurately estimate how many calories they should consume each day to maintain their weight. Consequently, these adults didn't know how many calories they should consume if they wanted to lose weight.

Thankfully, in these days of easy Internet information, it isn't very difficult to discover how many calories you need. So do the research and find your calorie target. Then, aim for the bull's-eye that leads to better health and a longer life.

WORKING IT OUT
PROCRASTINATION DOES NOT PAY

Healthy choices are easy to put off until some future date. But procrastination, especially concerning matters of personal health, is, at best, foolish and, at worst, dangerous. If you feel the need to improve your physical health, don't wait for New Year's Day; don't even wait until tomorrow. The time to begin living a healthier life is the moment you finish reading this sentence.

START MAKING CHANGES NOW

Warren Wiersbe correctly observed, "A Christian should no more defile his body than a Jew would defile the temple." Unfortunately, too many of us have allowed our temples to fall into disrepair. When it comes to fitness and food, it's easy to fall into bad habits. And it's easy to convince ourselves that we'll start improving our health "some day."

If we are to care for our bodies in the way that God intends, we must establish healthy habits, and we must establish them sooner rather than later.

Saint Jerome advised, "Begin to be now what you will be hereafter." You should take his advice seriously, and you should take it NOW. When it comes to your health, it's always the right time to start establishing the right habits.

STRENGTHENING YOUR FAITH
WHAT GOD WANTS FOR YOU

Since God loves you, and since He wants the very best for you, don't you believe that He also wants you to enjoy a healthy lifestyle? Of course He does. And since a healthy lifestyle is what God wants for you, isn't it what you should want, too?

MORE FROM GOD'S WORD ABOUT
THE SIMPLE LIFE

A simple life in the Fear-of-God is better than a rich life with a ton of headaches.

Proverbs 15:16 MSG

Do not love the world or the things in the world. If anyone loves the world, the love of the Father is not in him.

1 John 2:15 NKJV

We brought nothing into the world, so we can take nothing out. But, if we have food and clothes, we will be satisfied with that.

1 Timothy 6:7-8 NCV

So think clearly and exercise self-control. Look forward to the special blessings that will come to you at the return of Jesus Christ.

1 Peter 1:13 NLT

For the grace of God has been revealed, bringing salvation to all people. And we are instructed to turn from godless living and sinful pleasures. We should live in this evil world with self-control, right conduct, and devotion to God.

Titus 2:11-12 NLT

NOTES TO YOURSELF

Are your health-related goals clearly defined? Do you have a targeted level of exercise? And do you know how many calories you should be consuming each day based on your age, your health, and your activity level? If so, congratulations. If not, take time to learn how many calories you should be consuming each day. Then, take a few minutes to write down your health-related goals in the space below. Review these goals often.

_____

_____

_____

_____

_____

_____

_____

_____

_____

_____

RESPECTING YOUR BODY

Therefore, brothers, by the mercies of God,
I urge you to present your bodies as a living sacrifice,
holy and pleasing to God; this is your spiritual worship.

—

Romans 12:1 HCSB

THE BIBLICAL PRINCIPLE

If you're not determined to be
the master of your body . . . then you might just
become a slave to your impulses.

In the 12th chapter of Romans, Paul encourages us to make our bodies "holy and pleasing to God." Paul adds that to do so is a "spiritual act of worship." For believers, the implication is clear: God intends that we take special care of the bodies He has given us. But it's tempting to do otherwise.

We live in a fast-food world where unhealthy choices are convenient, inexpensive, and tempting. And, we live in a digital world filled with modern conveniences that often rob us of the physical exercise needed to maintain healthy lifestyles. As a result, too many of us find ourselves glued to the television, with a snack in one hand and a clicker in the other. The results are as unfortunate as they are predictable.

How do you treat your body? Do you treat it with the reverence and respect it deserves, or do you take it more or less for granted? Well, the Bible has clear instructions about the way you should take care of the miraculous body that God has given you.

God's Word teaches us that our bodies are "temples" that belong to God (1 Corinthians 6:19-20). We are commanded (not encouraged, not advised—we are commanded!) to treat our bodies with respect and honor. We do so by making wise choices and by making those choices consistently over an extended period of time.

MORE FROM GOD'S WORD

For we know that if our earthly house, a tent, is destroyed, we have a building from God, a house not made with hands, eternal in the heavens.

2 Corinthians 5:1 HCSB

For it was You who created my inward parts; You knit me together in my mother's womb. I will praise You, because I have been remarkably and wonderfully made.

Psalm 139:13-14 HCSB

Don't you know that you are God's sanctuary and that the Spirit of God lives in you?

1 Corinthians 3:16 HCSB

FOOD FOR THOUGHT
BECOME AN EDUCATED CONSUMER

Educate yourself on which foods are healthy and which foods aren't. Read labels and learn the basics of proper nutrition. Then, use common sense and discipline in planning your diet.

MORE THOUGHTS ABOUT
TAKING CARE OF YOUR BODY

Our body is like armor, our soul like the warrior. Take care of both, and you will be ready for what comes.

Amma St. Syncletice

Food ought to be a refreshment to the body, and not a burden.

St. Bonaventure

Eat to live, and not live to eat.

Poor Richard's Almanac

In general, mankind, since the improvement of cookery, eats twice as much as nature requires.

Ben Franklin

Attention to one's lifestyle, especially in the direction of reducing emotional tensions, a modest but regular program of daily exercise, a diet low in salt and sugar and reasonably free of fatty meats and fried foods, and plenty of good drinking water—all these are useful and indeed essential.

Norman Cousins

WHAT KIND OF EATER ARE YOU?

Take a few minutes to examine your eating habits. Do you gobble down snack foods while watching television? If so, stop. Do you drink high-calorie soft drinks or feast on unhealthy snacks like potato chips or candy? If so, you're doing yourself a disservice? Do you load up your plate and then feel obligated to eat every last bite? If so, it's time to form some new habits.

Poor eating habits are usually well established, so they won't be easy to change, but change them you must if you want to enjoy the benefits of a healthy lifestyle.

WORKING IT OUT
WHEN IT COMES TO EXERCISE,
PERSISTENCE PAYS

An exercise program that starts slowly and builds over time is far better than an exercise program that starts—and ends—quickly.

MAKING THE RIGHT CHOICES

Life is a series of choices. Each day, we make countless decisions that can bring us closer to God . . . or not. When we live according to God's commandments, we earn for ourselves the abundance and peace that He intends for us to experience. But, when we turn our backs upon God by disobeying Him, we bring needless suffering upon ourselves and our families.

Do you seek God's peace and His blessings? Then obey Him. When you're faced with a difficult choice or a powerful temptation, seek God's counsel and trust the counsel He gives. Invite God into your heart and live according to His commandments. When you do, you will be blessed today, tomorrow, and forever.

God has given you a guidebook for righteous living called the Holy Bible. It contains thorough instructions which, if followed, lead to fulfillment and salvation. But, if you choose to ignore God's commandments, the results are as predictable as they are tragic.

So here's a surefire formula for a happy, abundant life: live righteously.

And for further instructions, read the manual.

MORE FROM GOD'S WORD ABOUT RIGHTEOUSNESS

The righteous one will live by his faith.

Habakkuk 2:4 HCSB

Flee from youthful passions, and pursue righteousness, faith, love, and peace, along with those who call on the Lord from a pure heart.

2 Timothy 2:22 HCSB

And now, Israel, what does the Lord your God ask of you except to fear the Lord your God by walking in all His ways, to love Him, and to worship the Lord your God with all your heart and all your soul?

Deuteronomy 10:12 HCSB

STRENGTHENING YOUR FAITH
HAVE FAITH AND GET BUSY

Here's a time-tested formula for success: have faith in God and do the work. It has been said that there are no shortcuts to any place worth going, and those words apply to your physical fitness, too. There are simply no shortcuts to a healthy lifestyle.

NOTES TO YOURSELF

In the space below, make notes thanking God for the body
He has given you.

_____

_____

_____

_____

_____

_____

_____

_____

_____

_____

_____

_____

_____

_____

_____

_____

_____

THE RIGHT KIND OF EXERCISE FOR YOU

*He gives strength to the weary
and strengthens the powerless.*

———

Isaiah 40:29 HCSB

THE BIBLICAL PRINCIPLE

Your exercise regimen should be sensible,
enjoyable, safe, and consistent.

I f you want to attain and maintain a healthy lifestyle, it's important to engage in a consistent exercise program. Implementing a plan of regular, sensible exercise is one way of ensuring that you've done your part to care for the body that God has given you.

Dr. Kenneth Cooper observed, "Physical activity achieved at any level is an essential ingredient in slowing down the process of aging and turning life into a far more useful, enjoyable—and independent—affair." So what's the right kind of exercise for you? That's a question for you and your doctor. But whether you're running marathons or walking around the block, it's important to stay as active as you can, as long as you can.

No one can force you to exercise . . . you'll need to make that decision on your own. And if you genuinely desire to please God, it's a decision that you will make today.

FOOD FOR THOUGHT
MODERATION DAY BY DAY

John Maxwell observed, "The key to healthy eating is moderation and managing what you eat every day." And he was right. Crash diets don't usually work, but sensible eating habits do work, so plan your meals accordingly.

MORE FROM GOD'S WORD

And He said to me, "My grace is sufficient for you, for My strength is made perfect in weakness."

2 Corinthians 12:9 NKJV

You, therefore, my child, be strong in the grace that is in Christ Jesus.

2 Timothy 2:1 HCSB

The Lord is my strength and my song; He has become my salvation.

Exodus 15:2 HCSB

But those who wait on the Lord shall renew their strength; they shall mount up with wings like eagles, they shall run and not be weary, they shall walk and not faint.

Isaiah 40:31 NKJV

Finally, be strengthened by the Lord and by His vast strength.

Ephesians 6:10 HCSB

MORE THOUGHTS ABOUT
THE IMPORTANCE OF EXERCISE

People who exercise at least 3 hours a week tend to eat a more balanced and a healthier diet.

Dr. Walt Larimore

Give at least two hours every day to exercise, for health must not be sacrificed to learning. A strong body makes the mind strong.

Thomas Jefferson

It is remarkable how one's wits are sharpened by physical exercise.

Pliny the Younger

An early morning walk is a blessing for the whole day.

Henry David Thoreau

Fitness is a state of body and a state of mind: if your mind leads, your body will follow.

Marie T. Freeman

HOW MUCH EXERCISE?

How much exercise is right for you? That's a decision that you should make in consultation with your physician. But make no mistake: if you want to be a thoughtful caretaker of the only body you'll ever have in this world, exercise is important.

The benefits of exercise are not only physical but also psychological. Regular exercise allows you to build your muscles while you're clearing your head and lifting your spirits. So, if you're not already working out, talk to your doctor and then start an exercise regimen that's right for you. When you do, you'll be doing both your body and your mind a favor . . . and they'll both thank you for it.

WORKING IT OUT
REMAKE YOUR ENVIRONMENT

If you're trying to remodel yourself, you'll need to remodel your environment, too. In order to decrease temptations and increase the probability of success, you should take a long, hard look at your home, your office, and the places you frequently visit. Then, you must do whatever you can to move yourself as far as possible from the temptations that you intend to defeat.

SENSIBLE EXERCISE

A healthy lifestyle includes regular, sensible physical exercise. How much exercise is right for you? That's a decision that you should make in consultation with your physician. But make no mistake: if you sincerely desire to be a thoughtful caretaker of the body that God has given you, exercise is important.

Once you begin a regular exercise program, you'll discover that the benefits to you are not only physical but also psychological. Regular exercise allows you to build your muscles while you're clearing your head and lifting your spirits.

So, if you've been taking your body for granted, today is a wonderful day to change. You can start slowly, perhaps with a brisk walk around the block. As your stamina begins to build, so too will your sense of satisfaction. And, you'll be comforted by knowledge that you've done your part to protect and preserve the precious body that God has entrusted to your care.

MORE FROM GOD'S WORD ABOUT YOUR PRIORITIES

Don't abandon wisdom, and she will watch over you; love her, and she will guard you.

Proverbs 4:6 HCSB

And I pray this: that your love will keep on growing in knowledge and every kind of discernment, so that you can determine what really matters and can be pure and blameless in the day of Christ.

Philippians 1:9 HCSB

He said to them all, "If anyone desires to come after Me, let him deny himself, and take up his cross daily, and follow Me. For whoever desires to save his life will lose it, but whoever loses his life for My sake will save it."

Luke 9:23-24 NKJV

STRENGTHENING YOUR FAITH
GOD REWARDS OBEDIENCE

God's instructions are clear: He rewards wise behaviors and He punishes misbehavior. A commitment to a sensible program is one way of being wise, and it's also one way of pleasing God every day.

NOTES TO YOURSELF

In the space below, make notes about the spiritual, psychological, and physical benefits you experience when you exercise.

_____

_____

_____

_____

_____

_____

_____

_____

_____

_____

_____

_____

_____

PROTECTING YOUR EMOTIONAL HEALTH

*And the peace of God, which surpasses every thought,
will guard your hearts and your minds in Christ Jesus.
Finally brothers, whatever is true, whatever is honorable,
whatever is just, whatever is pure, whatever is lovely,
whatever is commendable—if there is any moral excellence
and if there is any praise—dwell on these things.*

—

Philippians 4:7-8 HCSB

THE BIBLICAL PRINCIPLE

When negative emotions threaten
to hijack your day, lift your thoughts—
and your prayers—to God.

Emotional health isn't simply the absence of sadness; it's also the ability to enjoy life and the wisdom to celebrate God's gifts. Christians have every reason to be optimistic about life. As John Calvin observed, "There is not one blade of grass, there is no color in this world that is not intended to make us rejoice." But sometimes, when we are tired or frustrated, rejoicing seems only a distant promise. Thankfully, God stands ready to restore us: "I will give you a new heart and put a new spirit in you" (Ezekiel 36:26 NIV). Our task, of course, is to let Him.

If you're feeling deeply discouraged or profoundly depressed, then it is time to seriously address the state of your emotional health. First, open your heart to God in prayer. Then, talk with trusted family members, friends, and your pastor. And, if you or someone close to you considers it wise, seek advice from your physician or make an appointment with a licensed mental health professional.

When your emotional health is at stake, you should avail yourself of every reasonable resource. Then, armed with the promises of your Creator and the support of family and friends, you can go about the business of solving the challenges that confront you. When you do, the clouds will eventually part, and the sun will shine once more upon your soul.

MORE FROM GOD'S WORD

Don't worry about your life, what you will eat or what you will drink; or about your body, what you will wear. Isn't life more than food and the body more than clothing?

Matthew 6:25 HCSB

Don't worry about anything, but in everything, through prayer and petition with thanksgiving, let your requests be made known to God.

Philippians 4:6 HCSB

Therefore don't worry about tomorrow, because tomorrow will worry about itself. Each day has enough trouble of its own.

Matthew 6:34 HCSB

FOOD FOR THOUGHT
WEIGHT LOSS MADE SIMPLE

It's really very simple: to lose weight, expend more energy and take in fewer calories. To gain weight, do the opposite. Likewise, the cure for obesity is also simple, but implementing that cure isn't. Weight loss requires lots of planning and lots of self-discipline. But with God's help, you're up to the task.

MORE THOUGHTS ABOUT
EMOTIONAL HEALTH

The busier we are, the easier it is to worry, the greater the temptation to worry, the greater the need to be alone with God.

Charles Stanley

We sometimes fear to bring our troubles to God because we think they must seem small to Him. But, if they are large enough to vex and endanger our welfare, they are large enough to touch His heart of love.

R. A. Torrey

A God wise enough to create me and the world that I live in is wise enough to watch out for me.

Philip Yancey

Worry does not empty tomorrow of its sorrow; it empties today of its strength.

Corrie ten Boom

The spiritual life is a life beyond moods. It is a life in which we choose joy and do not allow ourselves to become victims of passing feelings of happiness or depression.

Henri Nouwen

SADNESS VERSUS DEPRESSION

It's been said, and with good reason, that depression is the common cold of mental illness. Why? Because depression is such a common malady. But make no mistake: depression is a serious condition that, if untreated, can take a terrible toll on individuals and families alike.

The sadness that accompanies any significant loss is an inevitable fact of life. In time, sadness runs its course and gradually abates. Depression, on the other hand, is a physical and emotional condition that is, in almost all cases, treatable with medication and counseling. Depression is not a disease to be taken lightly. Left untreated, it presents real dangers to patients' physical health and to their emotional well-being.

If you find yourself feeling "blue," perhaps it's a logical reaction to the ups and downs of daily life. But if your feelings of sadness have gone on longer than you think they should—or if someone close to you fears that your sadness may have evolved into clinical depression—it's time to seek professional help. Consider the following:

1. If you have persistent urges toward self-destructive behavior, or if you feel as though you have lost the will to live, consult a professional counselor or physician immediately.

2. If someone you trust urges you to seek counseling, schedule a session with a professionally trained counselor to evaluate your condition.

3. If you experience persistent and prolonged changes in sleep patterns, or if you experience a significant change in weight (either gain or loss), consult your physician.

4. If you are plagued by consistent, prolonged, severe feelings of hopelessness, consult a physician or professional counselor.

In summary, depression is a serious but treatable condition. If you suspect that depression may have a grip on you or someone you love, seek professional guidance without delay.

WORKING IT OUT
WALK MORE, RIDE LESS

In earlier times, our forefathers (and mothers) walked a lot. In these times, we walk a little. Our ancestors had it right—walking is healthy, and most of us should walk much more than we do.

BUILDING HEALTHY RELATIONSHIPS

Emotional health is contagious, and so is emotional distress. If you're fortunate enough to be surrounded by family members and friends who celebrate life and praise God, consider yourself profoundly blessed. But, if you find yourself caught in an unhealthy relationship, it's time to look realistically at your situation and begin making changes.

Don't worry about changing other people: you can't do it. What you can do is to conduct yourself in a responsible fashion and insist that other people treat you with the dignity and consideration that you deserve.

In a perfect world filled with perfect people, our relationships, too, would be perfect. But none of us are perfect and neither are our relationships . . . and that's okay. As we work to make our imperfect relationships a little happier and healthier, we grow as individuals and as families. But, if we find ourselves in relationships that are debilitating or dangerous, then changes must be made, and soon.

If you find yourself caught up in a personal relationship that is bringing havoc into your life, and if you can't seem to find the courage to do something about it, don't hesitate to consult your pastor. Or, you may seek the advice of a trusted friend or a professionally trained counselor. But whatever you do, don't be satisfied with the status quo.

God has grand plans for your life; He has promised you the joy and abundance that can be yours through Him.

But to fully experience God's gifts, you need happy, emotionally healthy people to share them with. It's up to you to make sure that you do your part to build the kinds of relationships that will enrich your life and allow you to enrich the lives of your loved ones.

STRENGTHENING YOUR FAITH
CONTROLLABLE WORRIES ABOUT UNCONTROLLABLE PROBLEMS

Assiduously divide your areas of concern into two categories: those you can control and those you cannot. Then, do your best to refrain from wasting time or energy worrying about the latter.

MORE FROM GOD'S WORD ABOUT
THE DIRECTION OF YOUR THOUGHTS

Set your minds on what is above, not on what is on the earth.

Colossians 3:2 HCSB

Brothers, don't be childish in your thinking, but be infants in evil and adult in your thinking.

1 Corinthians 14:20 HCSB

Guard your heart above all else, for it is the source of life.

Proverbs 4:23 HCSB

May the words of my mouth and the meditation of my heart be acceptable to You, Lord, my rock and my Redeemer.

Psalm 19:14 HCSB

Commit your works to the Lord, and your thoughts will be established.

Proverbs 16:3 NKJV

NOTES TO YOURSELF

In the space below, write down at least three things you're worried about, and then ask God to help you turn those worries over to Him.

_____

_____

_____

_____

_____

_____

_____

_____

_____

_____

_____

_____

_____

_____

_____

_____

IT TAKES DISCIPLINE

*I am able to do all things
through Him who strengthens me.*

—

Philippians 4:13 HCSB

THE BIBLICAL PRINCIPLE

Discipline matters.
It takes discipline to strengthen your faith;
it takes discipline to improve your fitness.

Physical fitness requires discipline: the discipline to exercise regularly and the discipline to eat sensibly—it's as simple as that. But here's the catch: understanding the need for discipline is easy, but leading a disciplined life can be hard for most of us. Why? Because it's usually more fun to eat a second piece of cake than it is to jog a second lap around the track. But, as we survey the second helpings that all too often find their way onto our plates, we should consider this: as Christians, we are instructed to lead disciplined lives, and when we behave in undisciplined ways, we are living outside God's will.

God's Word reminds us again and again that our Creator expects us to be disciplined in our thoughts and disciplined in our actions. God doesn't reward laziness, misbehavior, apathy, or shortsightedness. To the contrary, He expects believers to behave with dignity and self-control.

We live in a world in which leisure is glorified and consumption is commercialized. But God has other plans. He did not create us for lives of gluttony or slothfulness; He created us for far greater things.

Life's greatest rewards seldom fall into our laps; to the contrary, our greatest accomplishments usually require lots of work, which is perfectly fine with God. After all, He knows that we're up to the task, and He has big plans for us; may we, as disciplined believers, always be worthy of those plans.

MORE FROM GOD'S WORD

No discipline seems enjoyable at the time, but painful. Later on, however, it yields the fruit of peace and righteousness to those who have been trained by it.

Hebrews 12:11 HCSB

The one who follows instruction is on the path to life, but the one who rejects correction goes astray.

Proverbs 10:17 HCSB

For this very reason, make every effort to supplement your faith with goodness, goodness with knowledge, knowledge with self-control, self-control with endurance, endurance with godliness.

2 Peter 1:5-6 HCSB

I discipline my body and bring it under strict control, so that after preaching to others, I myself will not be disqualified.

1 Corinthians 9:27 HCSB

Therefore by their fruits you will know them.

Matthew 7:20 NKJV

MORE THOUGHTS ABOUT DISCIPLINE

If one examines the secret behind a championship football team, a magnificent orchestra, or a successful business, the principal ingredient is invariably discipline.

James Dobson

Discipline is training that develops and corrects.

Charles Stanley

Work is doing it. Discipline is doing it every day. Diligence is doing it well every day.

Dave Ramsey

FOOD FOR THOUGHT
DISCIPLINE IS NOT A FOUR-LETTER WORD

Exercising discipline should never be viewed as an imposition or as a form of punishment; far from it. Discipline is the means by which you can take control of your life (which, by the way, is far better than letting your life control you).

THE SOURCE OF STRENGTH

Where do you go to find strength? The gym? The health food store? The espresso bar? There's a better source of strength, of course, and that source is God. He is a never-ending source of strength and courage if you call upon Him.

Are you an energized Christian? You should be. But if you're not, you must seek strength and renewal from the source that will never fail: that source, of course, is your Heavenly Father. And rest assured—when you sincerely petition Him, He will give you all the strength you need to live victoriously for Him.

Are you a woman who has "tapped in" to the power of God? Have you turned your life and your heart over to Him, or are you muddling along under your own power? The answer to this question will determine the quality of your life here on earth and the destiny of your life throughout all eternity. So start tapping in—and remember that when it comes to strength, God is the Ultimate Source.

God cannot build character without
our cooperation. If we resist Him,
then He chastens us into submission.
But, if we submit to Him, then He can
accomplish His work. He is not satisfied
with a halfway job. God wants a perfect work;
He wants a finished product
that is mature and complete.

—

Warren Wiersbe

WORKING IT OUT
START NOW

If you're genuinely planning on becoming a disciplined person "some day" in the distant future, you're deluding yourself. The best day to begin exercising self-discipline is this one.

SMALL STEPS

I f you want to become more physically fit, you don't have to make one giant leap. You can start with many small steps, and you should. When it comes to any new exercise regimen, starting slowly and improving gradually is the smart way to do it.

Crash diets usually crash. And fitness fads fade. But sensible exercise, when combined with a moderate diet, produces results that last.

So if you're determined to improve the state of your health, remember that consistency is the key. Start slowly, avoid injury, be consistent, and expect gradual improvement, not instant success.

STRENGTHENING YOUR FAITH
THE BOOK OF PROVERBS
HAS MUCH TO TEACH

If you're looking for words of wisdom that extol the virtues of a disciplined lifestyle, the Book of Proverbs is a wonderful place to start. It has 31 chapters, one for each day of the month. If you read Proverbs regularly, and if you take its teachings to heart, you'll become a more disciplined person. And God will smile.

MORE FROM GOD'S WORD ABOUT GOD'S STRENGTH

Be of good courage, and let us be strong for our people and for the cities of our God. And may the Lord do what is good in His sight.

1 Chronicles 19:13 NKJV

Do you not know? Have you not heard? The Everlasting God, the LORD, the Creator of the ends of the earth does not become weary or tired. His understanding is inscrutable. He gives strength to the weary, and to him who lacks might He increases power. Though youths grow weary and tired, and vigorous young men stumble badly, yet those who wait for the LORD will gain new strength; they will mount up with wings like eagles, they will run and not get tired, they will walk and not become weary.

Isaiah 40:28–31 NASB

The LORD is my strength and my song....

Exodus 15:2 NIV

The LORD is a refuge for His people and a stronghold.

Joel 3:16 NASB

NOTES TO YOURSELF

In the space below, make notes about small, but important, steps you can take to improve your health.

_____

_____

_____

_____

_____

_____

_____

_____

_____

_____

_____

_____

_____

_____

HEALTHY PRIORITIES

*Beloved, I pray that in all respects you may prosper
and be in good health, just as your soul prospers.*

—

3 John 1:2 NASB

THE BIBLICAL PRINCIPLE

Fitness is a journey, not a destination.
Achieving physical fitness—and maintaining it—
is a seven-day-a-week assignment.
If you don't make physical fitness a priority,
your health will suffer.

When it comes to matters of physical, spiritual, and emotional health, Christians possess an infallible guidebook: the Holy Bible. And, when it comes to matters concerning fitness—whether physical, emotional, or spiritual fitness—God's Word can help us establish clear priorities that can guide our steps and our lives.

It's easy to talk about establishing clear priorities for maintaining physical and spiritual health, but it's much more difficult to live according to those priorities. For busy believers living in a demanding world, placing first things first can be difficult indeed. Why? Because so many people are expecting so many things from us!

If you're having trouble prioritizing your day—or if you're having trouble sticking to a plan that enhances your spiritual and physical health—perhaps you've been trying to organize your life according to your own plans, not God's. A better strategy, of course, is to take your daily obligations and place them in the hands of the One who created you. To do so, you must prioritize your day according to God's commandments, and you must seek His will and His wisdom in all matters.

Would you like to embark upon a personal journey to better fitness? If so, you should remind yourself that on every step of that journey, you have a traveling companion: your Heavenly Father. Turn the concerns of this day over to Him—prayerfully, earnestly, and often. And trust Him to give you the strength you need to become the kind of person He wants you to become.

FOOD FOR THOUGHT
BECOME AN EXPERT

You don't have to attend medical school to understand the basic principles of maintaining a healthy lifestyle. In fact, many of the things you need to know are contained in this text. But don't stop here. Vow to make yourself an expert on the care and feeding of the body that God has given you. In today's information-packed world, becoming an expert isn't a very hard thing to do.

MORE FROM GOD'S WORD

Do you not know that your body is a sanctuary of the Holy Spirit who is in you, whom you have from God? You are not your own, for you were bought at a price; therefore glorify God in your body.

1 Corinthians 6:19-20 HCSB

I have come that they may have life, and that they may have it more abundantly.

John 10:10 NKJV

I urge you to live a life worthy of the calling you have received.

Ephesians 4:1 NIV

My cup runs over. Surely goodness and mercy shall follow me all the days of my life; and I will dwell in the house of the Lord forever.

Psalm 23:5-6 NKJV

Is any among you afflicted? Let him pray.

James 5:13 KJV

MORE THOUGHTS ABOUT HEALTH

The soul is the user, the body for use; hence the one is master, the other servant.

St. Ambrose of Milan

Ultimate healing and the glorification of the body are certainly among the blessings of Calvary for the believing Christian. Immediate healing is not guaranteed.

Warren Wiersbe

Let exercise alternate with rest.

Pythagoras

The effective Christians of history have been men and women of great personal discipline—mental discipline, discipline of the body, discipline of the tongue, and discipline of the emotion.

Billy Graham

Exercise: you don't have time not to.

Anonymous

KNOW YOUR BLOOD PRESSURE

High blood pressure can cause heart attacks, strokes, and plenty of other serious health problems. The good news is that high blood pressure is usually treatable with medication, or lifestyle changes, or both. But you won't know you need treatment unless you know your blood pressure. Thankfully, blood pressure cuffs can be found just about everywhere, in many drug stores and even in some supermarkets. Or, if you prefer, you can buy your own blood pressure cuff to use at home.

So remember this: you don't have to wait for a doctor's appointment to check your blood pressure. You can monitor your own blood pressure in between visits to the doctor's office, and that's precisely what you should do.

WORKING IT OUT
MAKE EXERCISE FUN

Make exercise enjoyable. Your workouts should be a source of pleasure and satisfaction, not a form of self-imposed punishment. Find a way to exercise your body that is satisfying, effective, and fun.

THE GIFT OF LIFE

Life is a glorious gift from God. Treat it that way. This day, like every other, is filled to the brim with opportunities, challenges, and choices. But, no choice that you make is more important than the choice you make concerning God. Today, you will either place Him at the center of your life—or not—and the consequences of that choice have implications that are both temporal and eternal.

Sometimes, we don't intentionally neglect God; we simply allow ourselves to become overwhelmed with the demands of everyday life. And then, without our even realizing it, we gradually drift away from the One we need most. Thankfully, God never drifts away from us. He remains always present, always steadfast, always loving.

As you begin this day, place God and His Son where they belong: in your head, in your prayers, on your lips, and in your heart. And then, with God as your guide and companion, let the journey begin . . .

MORE FROM GOD'S WORD ABOUT LIFE

I urge you now to live the life to which God called you.

Ephesians 4:1 NKJV

Rejoice in the Lord always. Again I will say, rejoice!

Philippians 4:4 NKJV

Jesus told him, "I am the way, the truth, and the life. No one comes to the Father except through Me."

John 14:6 HCSB

He who follows righteousness and mercy finds life, righteousness and honor.

Proverbs 21:21 NKJV

STRENGTHENING YOUR FAITH
DON'T TRUST THE MEDIA'S MESSAGES

Many of the messages that you receive from the media are specifically designed to sell you products that interfere with your spiritual, physical, or emotional health. God takes great interest in your health; the moguls from Madison Avenue take great interest in your pocketbook. Trust God.

NOTES TO YOURSELF

In the space below, write down ways that you can be more proactive about your health.

YOUR CHOICES MATTER

I am offering you life or death, blessings or curses.
Now, choose life! . . . To choose life is to love
the Lord your God, obey him, and stay close to him.

—

Deuteronomy 30:19-20 NCV

THE BIBLICAL PRINCIPLE

First you make choices . . . and soon
those choices begin to shape your life.
That's why you must make wise choices . . .
or face the consequences of
making unwise ones.

Each day, we make thousands of small choices concerning the things that we do and the things we think. Most of these choices are made without too much forethought. In fact, most of us go about our daily lives spending a significant portion simply reacting to events. Often, our actions are simply the result of impulse or habit. God asks that we slow down long enough to think about the choices that we make, and He asks that we make those choices in accordance with His commandments.

The Bible teaches us that our bodies are "temples" that belong to God (1 Corinthians 6:19-20). We are commanded (not encouraged, not advised, commanded!) to treat our bodies with respect and honor. We do so by making wise choices and by making those choices consistently over an extended period of time.

Do you sincerely seek to improve the overall quality of your health? Then vow to yourself and to God that you will begin making the kind of wise choices that will lead to a longer, healthier, happier life. The responsibility for those choices is yours. And so are the rewards.

MORE FROM GOD'S WORD

So I strive always to keep my conscience clear before God and man.

Acts 24:16 NIV

The thing you should want most is God's kingdom and doing what God wants. Then all these other things you need will be given to you.

Matthew 6:33 NCV

Above all and before all, do this: Get Wisdom! Write this at the top of your list: Get Understanding!

Proverbs 4:7 MSG

FOOD FOR THOUGHT
IF SOMEONE ELSE
IS COOKING YOUR MEALS . . .

If someone else is cooking your meals, ask that person to help you plan a healthier diet. Without the cooperation of the person who cooks your food, you'll have an incredibly difficult time sticking to a healthier diet.

MORE THOUGHTS ABOUT
MAKING WISE CHOICES

Since behaviors become habits, make them work with you and not against you.

E. Stanley Jones

He who does not overcome small faults, shall fall little by little into greater ones.

Thomas à Kempis

There may be no trumpet sound or loud applause when we make a right decision, just a calm sense of resolution and peace.

Gloria Gaither

I do not know how the Spirit of Christ performs it, but He brings us choices through which we constantly change, fresh and new, into His likeness.

Joni Eareckson Tada

Life is a series of choices between the bad, the good, and the best. Everything depends on how we choose.

Vance Havner

EAT LESS, WALK MORE

Are you chained to a desk or trapped in a sedentary lifestyle? And are you waiting for something big to happen before you revolutionize your exercise habits? If so, wait no more. In fact, you can start today by substituting a light snack and a healthy walk for that calorie-laden lunch.

If you're in reasonably good shape, a nice healthy walk can be a great substitute for a big sit-down meal. So don't underestimate the benefits of a good walk. It's a great way to burn a few calories, to get some fresh air, and to improve your life.

WORKING IT OUT
MANY CHANCES
TO MAKE GOOD DECISIONS

Physical fitness is not the result of a single decision that is made "once and for all." Physical fitness results from thousands of decisions that are made day after day, week after week, and year after year.

ALWAYS KEEP LEARNING

Today is your classroom: what will you learn? Will you use today's experiences as tools for personal, spiritual, and physical improvement, or will you ignore the lessons that life and God are trying to teach you? Will you carefully study God's Word, and will you apply His teachings to the experiences of everyday life? The events of today have much to teach. You have much to learn. May you live—and learn—accordingly.

STRENGTHENING YOUR FAITH
HIGH-QUALITY CHOICES LEAD TO A HIGH-QUALITY LIFE

Every step of your life's journey is a choice . . . and the quality of those choices determines the quality of the journey.

MORE FROM GOD'S WORD ABOUT
LIFETIME LEARNING

If you listen to correction to improve your life, you will live among the wise.

Proverbs 15:31 NCV

Remember what you are taught, and listen carefully to words of knowledge.

Proverbs 23:12 NCV

The fear of the Lord is the beginning of knowledge, but fools despise wisdom and discipline.

Proverbs 1:7 NIV

The knowledge of the secrets of the kingdom of heaven has been given to you....

Matthew 13:11 NIV

It is not good to have zeal without knowledge, nor to be hasty and miss the way.

Proverbs 19:2 NIV

NOTES TO YOURSELF

In the space below, make a short list of people whose healthy habits you admire. Then, jot down a few things you can do to become a little more like them.

_____

_____

_____

_____

_____

_____

_____

_____

_____

_____

_____

_____

_____

_____

_____

_____

BEYOND THE SETBACKS

Peace, peace to you, and peace to him who helps you,
for your God helps you.

—

1 Chronicles 12:18 HCSB

THE BIBLICAL PRINCIPLE

Time and again, the Bible preaches
the power of perseverance.
Setbacks, disappointments, and failures are inevitable—
your response to them is optional.
If you don't give up, you can turn
your stumbling blocks into stepping stones.

I t's simply a fact of life: Not all of your health-related plans will succeed, and not all of your goals will be met. Life's occasional setbacks are simply the price that we must pay for our willingness to take risks as we follow our dreams. But even when we encounter bitter disappointments, we must never lose faith.

Hebrews 10:36 advises, "Patient endurance is what you need now, so you will continue to do God's will. Then you will receive all that he has promised" (NLT). These words remind us that when we persevere, we will eventually receive the rewards which God has promised us. What's required is perseverance, not perfection.

When we face hardships, God stands ready to protect us. Our responsibility, of course, is to ask Him for protection. When we call upon Him in heartfelt prayer, He will answer—in His own time and according to His own plan—and He will do His part to heal us. We, of course, must do our part, too.

And, while we are waiting for God's plans to unfold and for His healing touch to restore us, we can be comforted in the knowledge that our Creator can overcome any obstacle, even if we cannot.

MORE FROM GOD'S WORD

If we confess our sins to him, he is faithful and just to forgive us and to cleanse us from every wrong.

1 John 1:9 NLT

If you hide your sins, you will not succeed. If you confess and reject them, you will receive mercy.

Proverbs 28:13 NCV

If you listen to constructive criticism, you will be at home among the wise.

Proverbs 15:31 NLT

So we're not giving up. How could we! Even though on the outside it often looks like things are falling apart on us, on the inside, where God is making new life, not a day goes by without his unfolding grace.

2 Corinthians 4:16 MSG

I waited patiently for the LORD; he turned to me and heard my cry. He lifted me out of the slimy pit, out of the mud and mire; he set my feet on a rock and gave me a firm place to stand. He put a new song in my mouth, a hymn of praise to our God....

Psalm 40:1-3 NIV

MORE THOUGHTS ABOUT FAILURE

The enemy of our souls loves to taunt us with past failures, wrongs, disappointments, disasters, and calamities. And if we let him continue doing this, our life becomes a long and dark tunnel, with very little light at the end.

Charles Swindoll

What may seem defeat to us may be victory to him.

C. H. Spurgeon

Success or failure can be pretty well predicted by the degree to which the heart is fully in it.

John Eldredge

Never imagine that you can be a loser by trusting in God.

C. H. Spurgeon

The difference between winning and losing is how we choose to react to disappointment.

Barbara Johnson

NOTES TO YOURSELF

In the space below, make a few notes about the importance of perseverance and the rewards of persistence.

SO MANY TEMPTATIONS

The LORD is my strength and song,
and He has become my salvation;
He is my God, and I will praise Him . . .

———

Exodus 15:2 NKJV

THE BIBLICAL PRINCIPLE

In today's world, the temptations are great,
but with God's help, you can resist them.

It's inevitable: today you will be tempted by somebody or something—in fact, you will probably be tempted many times. Why? Because you live in a world that is filled to the brim with temptations! Some of these temptations are small; eating a second scoop of ice cream, for example, is enticing but not very dangerous. Other temptations, however, are not nearly so harmless.

The devil is working 24/7, and he's causing pain and heartache in more ways than ever before. We, as believers, must remain watchful and strong. And the good news is this: When it comes to fighting Satan, we are never alone. God is always with us, and He gives us the power to resist temptation whenever we ask Him to give us strength.

In a letter to believers, Peter offered a stern warning: "Your adversary, the devil, prowls around like a roaring lion, seeking someone to devour" (1 Peter 5:8 NASB). As Christians, we must take that warning seriously, and we must behave accordingly.

It is easier to stay out of temptation
than to get out of it.

—

Rick Warren

MORE FROM GOD'S WORD

No temptation has seized you except what is common to man. And God is faithful; he will not let you be tempted beyond what you can bear. But when you are tempted, he will also provide a way out so that you can stand up under it.

1 Corinthians 10:13 NIV

Be sober, be vigilant; because your adversary the devil walks about like a roaring lion, seeking whom he may devour.

1 Peter 5:8 NKJV

The Lord knows how to deliver the godly out of temptations.

2 Peter 2:9 NKJV

Put on the whole armor of God, that you may be able to stand against the wiles of the devil.

Ephesians 6:11 NKJV

This High Priest of ours understands our weaknesses, for he faced all of the same temptations we do, yet he did not sin.

Hebrews 4:15 NLT

MORE THOUGHTS ABOUT
TEMPTATION

Our battles are first won or lost in the secret places of our will in God's presence, never in full view of the world.

Oswald Chambers

God wants to reveal Himself as your heavenly Father. When you wonder which way to turn, you can grasp His strong hand, and He'll guide you along life's path.

Lisa Whelchel

Do not fight the temptation in detail. Turn from it. Look ONLY at your Lord. Sing. Read. Work.

Amy Carmichael

Temptation is not a sin. Even Jesus was tempted. The Lord Jesus gives you the strength needed to resist temptation.

Corrie ten Boom

Measure the size of the obstacles against the size of God.

Beth Moore

NOTES TO YOURSELF

In the space below, make notes about the ways that your spiritual, emotional, and physical health are interconnected.

_____

_____

_____

_____

_____

_____

_____

_____

_____

_____

_____

_____

_____

_____

YOUR BODY,
YOUR CHOICES

So then each of us shall give account of himself to God.

—

Romans 14:12 NKJV

THE BIBLICAL PRINCIPLE

You're the human being whom God
has entrusted with the responsibility of caring
for your body. So it's always the right time
to become proactive about your health.

As adults, each of us bears a personal responsibility for the general state of our own physical health. Certainly, various aspects of health are beyond our control: illness sometimes strikes even the healthiest men and women. But for most of us, physical health is a choice: it is the result of hundreds of small decisions that we make every day of our lives. If we make decisions that promote good health, our bodies respond. But if we fall into bad habits and undisciplined lifestyles, we suffer tragic consequences.

When our unhealthy habits lead to poor health, we find it all too easy to look beyond ourselves and assign blame. In fact, we live in a society where blame has become a national obsession: we blame cigarette manufacturers, restaurants, and food producers, to name only a few. But to blame others is to miss the point: we, and we alone, are responsible for the way that we treat our bodies. And the sooner that we accept that responsibility, the sooner we can assert control over our bodies and our lives.

Do you sincerely desire to improve your physical fitness? If so, start by taking personal responsibility for the body that God has given you. Then, make the solemn pledge to yourself that you will begin to make the changes that are required to enjoy a longer, healthier, happier life.

MORE FROM GOD'S WORD

Even a child is known by his actions, by whether his conduct is pure and right.

Proverbs 20:11 NIV

Light shines on the godly, and joy on those who do right. May all who are godly be happy in the Lord and praise his holy name.

Psalm 97:11-12 NLT

So teach us to number our days, that we may gain a heart of wisdom.

Psalm 90:12 NKJV

FOOD FOR THOUGHT
ACCEPT RESPONSIBILITY

It's easy to blame other people for the current state of your health. You live in a world where it's fashionable to blame food manufacturers, doctors, and fast-food restaurants, to mention but a few. Yet none of these folks force food into your mouth, and they don't force you to sit on the sofa when you should be exercising! So remember: it's your body . . . and it's your responsibility.

MORE THOUGHTS ABOUT TAKING RESPONSIBILITY

If you don't take care of your body, how can you expect your body to take care of you?

Marie T. Freeman

As we make an offering of our work, we find the truth of a principle Jesus taught: Fulfillment is not a goal to achieve, but always the by-product of a sacrifice.

Elisabeth Elliot

Although God causes all things to work together for good for His children, He still holds us accountable for our behavior.

Kay Arthur

Whether we know it or not, whether we agree with it or not, whether we practice it or not, whether we like it or not, we are accountable to one another.

Charles Stanley

Action springs not from thought, but from a readiness for responsibility.

Dietrich Bonhoeffer

THE FUTILITY OF BLAME

When our unhealthy habits lead to poor health, we find it all too easy to look beyond ourselves and assign blame. Why? Because blaming is much easier than fixing, and criticizing others is so much easier than improving ourselves. So instead of solving our problems legitimately (by doing the work required to solve them), we are inclined to fret, to blame, and to criticize, while doing precious little else. When we do, our problems, quite predictably, remain unsolved.

So, when it comes to your own body, assume control and accept responsibility. It's a great way to live and a great way to stay healthy.

WORKING IT OUT
GOOD INTENTIONS ARE NOT ENOUGH

The road to poor health is paved with good intentions. Until you make exercise a high priority in your life, your good intentions will soon give way to old habits. So give your exercise regimen a position of high standing on your daily to-do list.

BEWARE THE CHECKOUT LINE

Unless you're a hermit living on a deserted island, you pass through those check-out lines awash in tabloids and tasty treats. Of course, the retailers' strategy is straightforward: to get you to make a quick impulse purchase. So most times, you'll come face-to-face with an assortment of candies, chips, and pre-packed cookies. What's needed by you is willpower. Otherwise, you'll form the habit of impulsively munching on fat-laden, life-shortening snacks.

So here's your rule for the checkout lines of life: yield not to temptation. Keep your eyes and your hands to yourself, and leave all those unhealthy snacks on the shelf . . . or else.

STRENGTHENING YOUR FAITH
BUILDING A BETTER SELF-IMAGE

When you accept responsibilities and fulfill them, you'll feel better about yourself. When you avoid your obligations, you won't. Act accordingly.

MORE FROM GOD'S WORD ABOUT
DOING THE RIGHT THING

The righteous one will live by his faith.

Habakkuk 2:4 HCSB

And the world is passing away, and the lust of it; but he who does the will of God abides forever.

1 John 2:17 NKJV

Because the eyes of the Lord are on the righteous and His ears are open to their request. But the face of the Lord is against those who do evil.

1 Peter 3:12 HCSB

Flee from youthful passions, and pursue righteousness, faith, love, and peace, along with those who call on the Lord from a pure heart.

2 Timothy 2:22 HCSB

Sow righteousness for yourselves and reap faithful love; break up your untilled ground. It is time to seek the Lord until He comes and sends righteousness on you like the rain.

Hosea 10:12 HCSB

NOTES TO YOURSELF

In the space below, write down at least three things you need to take responsibility for today.

_____

_____

_____

_____

_____

_____

_____

_____

_____

_____

_____

_____

_____

_____

_____

ENTRUSTING YOUR HOPES TO GOD

*You, Lord, give true peace to those who depend on you,
because they trust you.*

—

Isaiah 26:3 NCV

THE BIBLICAL PRINCIPLE

Since God has promised to guide and protect you—
now and forever—you should never lose hope.

As every woman knows, hope is a perishable commodity. Despite God's promises, despite Christ's love, and despite our countless blessings, we are fallible human beings who can still lose hope from time to time. When we do, we need the encouragement of Christian friends, the life-changing power of prayer, and the healing truth of God's Holy Word.

As grateful servants of Christ, we should seek to cultivate our hopes each day through quiet meditation, through devotion to God, and through association with fellow believers. But sometimes, amid the hustle and bustle of everyday living, we leave our hopes to fend for themselves, and when we do, bad things begin to happen. If we find ourselves falling into the spiritual traps of worry and discouragement, we should seek the healing touch of Jesus and the encouraging words of fellow believers.

This world can be a place of trials and tribulations, yet we need never lose hope. God has promised us peace, joy, and eternal life—and God always keeps His promises. Always.

Never yield to gloomy anticipation.
Place your hope and confidence in God.
He has no record of failure.

—

Mrs. Charles E. Cowman

MORE FROM GOD'S WORD

Let us hold on to the confession of our hope without wavering, for He who promised is faithful.

Hebrews 10:23 HCSB

Hope deferred makes the heart sick.

Proverbs 13:12 NKJV

Sustain me as You promised, and I will live; do not let me be ashamed of my hope.

Psalm 119:116 HCSB

For I know the thoughts that I think toward you, says the Lord, thoughts of peace and not of evil, to give you a future and a hope. Then you will call upon Me and go and pray to Me, and I will listen to you.

Jeremiah 29:11-12 NKJV

Be of good courage, and He shall strengthen your heart, all you who hope in the Lord.

Psalm 31:24 NKJV

MORE THOUGHTS ABOUT HOPE

The best we can hope for in this life is a knothole peek at the shining realities ahead. Yet a glimpse is enough. It's enough to convince our hearts that whatever sufferings and sorrows currently assail us aren't worthy of comparison to that which waits over the horizon.

Joni Eareckson Tada

When you and I are related to Jesus Christ, our strength and wisdom and peace and joy and love and hope may run out, but His life rushes in to keep us filled to the brim. We are showered with blessings, not because of anything we have or have not done, but simply because of Him.

Anne Graham Lotz

Oh, remember this: There is never a time when we may not hope in God. Whatever our necessities, however great our difficulties, and though to all appearance help is impossible, yet our business is to hope in God, and it will be found that it is not in vain.

George Mueller

Teach us to set our hopes on heaven, to hold firmly to the promise of eternal life, so that we can withstand the struggles and storms of this world.

Max Lucado

NOTES TO YOURSELF

In the space below, write down a few of your thoughts about God's faithfulness, God's love, and God's promise of eternal life.

_____

_____

_____

_____

_____

_____

_____

_____

_____

_____

_____

_____

_____

_____

THE POWER OF OPTIMISM

*I am able to do all things through Him
who strengthens me.*

—

Philippians 4:13 HCSB

THE BIBLICAL PRINCIPLE

Optimism pays. Pessimism does not.
Guard your thoughts and your words accordingly.

As each day unfolds, you are quite literally surrounded by more opportunities than you can count—opportunities to improve your own spiritual, physical, and emotional health. God's Word promises that you, like all of His children, possess the ability to experience earthly peace and spiritual abundance. Yet sometimes—especially if you dwell upon the inevitable disappointments that may, at times, befall even the luckiest among us—you may allow pessimism to invade your thoughts and your heart.

The self-fulfilling prophecy is alive, well, and living at your house. If you constantly anticipate the worst, that's what you're likely to attract. But, if you make the effort to think positive thoughts, you'll increase the probability that those positive thoughts will come true.

So here's a simple, character-building tip for improving your life: put the self-fulfilling prophecy to work for you. Expect the best, and then get busy working to achieve it. When you do, you'll not only increase the odds of achieving your dreams, but you'll also have more fun along the way.

Developing a positive attitude means working
continually to find what is uplifting and encouraging.

—

Barbara Johnson

MORE FROM GOD'S WORD

Make me hear joy and gladness.

Psalm 51:8 NKJV

For God has not given us a spirit of fearfulness, but one of power, love, and sound judgment.

2 Timothy 1:7 HCSB

My cup runs over. Surely goodness and mercy shall follow me all the days of my life; and I will dwell in the house of the Lord Forever.

Psalm 23:5-6 NKJV

Let us hold on to the confession of our hope without wavering, for He who promised is faithful.

Hebrews 10:23 HCSB

But if we hope for what we do not see, we eagerly wait for it with patience.

Romans 8:25 HCSB

MORE THOUGHTS ABOUT OPTIMISM

The popular idea of faith is of a certain obstinate optimism: the hope, tenaciously held in the face of trouble, that the universe is fundamentally friendly and things may get better.

J. I. Packer

It is a remarkable thing that some of the most optimistic and enthusiastic people you will meet are those who have been through intense suffering.

Warren Wiersbe

Christ can put a spring in your step and a thrill in your heart. Optimism and cheerfulness are products of knowing Christ.

Billy Graham

The essence of optimism is that it takes no account of the present, but it is a source of inspiration, of vitality, and of hope. Where others have resigned, it enables a man to hold his head high, to claim the future for himself, and not abandon it to his enemy.

Dietrich Bonhoeffer

NOTES TO YOURSELF

In the space below, jot down a few ideas about the ways that an optimistic outlook might be beneficial to your spiritual, mental, and physical health.

ASKING FOR GOD'S HELP

So I say to you, ask, and it will be given to you;
seek, and you will find; knock, and it will be opened to you.
For everyone who asks receives, and he who seeks finds,
and to him who knocks it will be opened.

—

Luke 11:9-10 NKJV

THE BIBLICAL PRINCIPLE

If you're serious about improving your fitness or
your faith, you should pray about it.

D o you genuinely want to strengthen your fitness and your faith? If the answer to that question is yes, then you should set aside ample time each morning to ask for God's help.

Is prayer an integral part of your daily life, or is it a hit-or-miss habit? Do you "pray without ceasing," or is your prayer life an afterthought? Do you regularly pray in the quiet moments of the early morning, or do you bow your head only when others are watching?

As Christians, we are instructed to pray often. But it is important to note that genuine prayer requires much more than bending our knees and closing our eyes. Heartfelt prayer is an attitude of the heart.

If your prayers have become more a matter of habit than a matter of passion, you're robbing yourself of a deeper relationship with God. And how can you rectify that situation? By praying more frequently and more fervently. When you do, God will shower you with His blessings, His grace, and His love.

Too many of us, even well-intentioned believers, tend to "compartmentalize" our waking hours into a few familiar categories: work, rest, play, family time, and worship. To do so is a mistake. Worship and praise should be woven into the fabric of our lives; prayer should never be relegated to a weekly three-hour visit to church on Sunday morning.

Theologian Wayne Oates once admitted, "Many of my prayers are made with my eyes open. You see, it seems I'm always praying about something, and it's not always convenient—or safe—to close my eyes." Dr. Oates understood that God always hears our prayers and that the relative position of our eyelids is of no concern to Him.

Today, find a little more time to lift your concerns to God in prayer and praise.

FOOD FOR THOUGHT
PRAY ABOUT YOUR HEALTH

As you petition God each morning, ask Him for the strength and the wisdom to treat your body as His creation and His "temple." During the day ahead, you will face countless temptations to do otherwise, but with God's help, you can treat your body as the priceless, one-of-a-kind gift that it most certainly is.

MORE FROM GOD'S WORD

The intense prayer of the righteous is very powerful.

James 5:16 HCSB

Let the words of my mouth and the meditation of my heart be acceptable in Your sight, O Lord, my strength and my Redeemer.

Psalm 19:14 NKJV

Yet He often withdrew to deserted places and prayed.

Luke 5:16 HCSB

Rejoice in hope; be patient in affliction; be persistent in prayer.

Romans 12:12 HCSB

Is anyone among you suffering? He should pray. Is anyone cheerful? He should sing praises.

James 5:13 HCSB

MORE THOUGHTS ABOUT
THE POWER OF PRAYER

What God gives in answer to our prayers will always be the thing we most urgently need, and it will always be sufficient.

Elisabeth Elliot

God says we don't need to be anxious about anything; we just need to pray about everything.

Stormie Omartian

Are you weak? Weary? Confused? Troubled? Pressured? How is your relationship with God? Is it held in its place of priority? I believe the greater the pressure, the greater your need for time alone with Him.

Kay Arthur

When there is a matter that requires definite prayer, pray until you believe God and until you can thank Him for His answer.

Hannah Whitall Smith

ASK FOR GOD'S HELP

God wants you to experience abundant life, but He will not force you to adopt a healthy lifestyle. Managing your food and your fitness is up to you.

If you want more from life, ask more from God. D. L. Moody observed, "Some people think God does not like to be troubled with our constant asking. But, the way to trouble God is not to come at all." So, if you seek an improved level of fitness—or if you seek any other worthy goal—ask God (and keep asking Him) until He answers your prayers.

WORKING IT OUT
DAY IN, DAY OUT

Your journey with God unfolds day by day, and that's precisely how your journey to an improved state of physical fitness must also unfold: moment by moment, day by day, year by year.

PRAY CONSTANTLY

God's Word promises that prayer is a powerful tool for changing your life and your world. So here's a question: Are you using prayer as a powerful tool to improve your world, or are you praying sporadically at best? If you're wise, you've learned that prayer is indeed powerful and that it is most powerful when it is used often.

Today, if you haven't already done so, establish the habit of praying constantly. Don't pray day-to-day; pray hour-to-hour. Start each day with prayer, end it with prayer, and fill it with prayer. That's the best way to know God; it's the best way to change your world; and it is, quite simply, the best way to live.

STRENGTHENING YOUR FAITH
ASK MORE FREQUENTLY

If life's inevitable temptations seem to be getting the best of you, try praying more often, even if many of those prayers are simply brief, "open-eyed" requests to your Father in heaven.

MORE FROM GOD'S WORD ABOUT
ASKING FOR GOD'S HELP

If you remain in Me and My words remain in you, ask whatever you want and it will be done for you.

John 15:7 HCSB

What father among you, if his son asks for a fish, will, instead of a fish, give him a snake? Or if he asks for an egg, will give him a scorpion? If you then, who are evil, know how to give good gifts to your children, how much more will the heavenly Father give the Holy Spirit to those who ask Him?

Luke 11:11-13 HCSB

Don't worry about anything, but in everything, through prayer and petition with thanksgiving, let your requests be made known to God.

Philippians 4:6 HCSB

You do not have because you do not ask.

James 4:2 HCSB

For the Lord gives wisdom; from His mouth come knowledge and understanding.

Proverbs 2:6 NKJV

NOTES TO YOURSELF

In the space below, make notes about the things you need
to pray about today.

_____

_____

_____

_____

_____

_____

_____

_____

_____

_____

_____

_____

_____

_____

SPIRITUAL HEALTH, SPIRITUAL GROWTH

*But the fruit of the Spirit is love, joy, peace,
long-suffering, gentleness, goodness, faith,
meekness, temperance . . . .*

—

Galatians 5:22-23 KJV

THE BIBLICAL PRINCIPLE

Wherever you are in your spiritual journey,
it's always the right time
to take another step toward God.

A re you as "spiritually fit" as you're ever going to be? Hopefully not! When it comes to your faith (and, by the way, when it comes to your fitness), God isn't done with you yet.

The journey toward spiritual maturity lasts a lifetime: As Christians, we can and should continue to grow in the love and the knowledge of our Savior as long as we live. But, if we cease to grow, either emotionally or spiritually, we do ourselves and our families a profound disservice.

If we study God's Word, if we obey His commandments, and if we live in the center of His will, we will not be "stagnant" believers; we will, instead, be growing Christians . . . and that's exactly what God wants for our lives.

In those quiet moments when we open our hearts to God, the Creator who made us keeps remaking us. He gives us direction, perspective, wisdom, and courage. He encourages us to become more fit in a variety of ways: more spiritually fit, more physically fit, and more emotionally fit.

God is willing to do His part to ensure that you remain fit. Are you willing to do yours?

MORE FROM GOD'S WORD

For this reason also, since the day we heard this, we haven't stopped praying for you. We are asking that you may be filled with the knowledge of His will in all wisdom and spiritual understanding.

Colossians 1:9 HCSB

Therefore, leaving the elementary message about the Messiah, let us go on to maturity.

Hebrews 6:1 HCSB

But grow in the grace and knowledge of our Lord and Savior Jesus Christ. To Him be the glory both now and to the day of eternity.

2 Peter 3:18 HCSB

FOOD FOR THOUGHT
IT TAKES TIME

Spiritual growth is not instantaneous . . . and neither, for that matter, is the attainment of a physically fit body. So be patient. You should expect a few ups and downs along the way, but you should also expect to see progress over time.

MORE THOUGHTS ABOUT
SPIRITUAL GROWTH

When you and I hurt deeply, what we really need is not an explanation from God but a revelation of God. We need to see how great God is; we need to recover our lost perspective on life. Things get out of proportion when we are suffering, and it takes a vision of something bigger than ourselves to get life's dimensions adjusted again.

Warren Wiersbe

We set our eyes on the finish line, forgetting the past, and straining toward the mark of spiritual maturity and fruitfulness.

Vonette Bright

You are either becoming more like Christ every day or you're becoming less like Him. There is no neutral position in the Lord.

Stormie Omartian

A Christian is never in a state of completion but always in the process of becoming.

Martin Luther

PERFECTION? FORGET ABOUT IT

As you begin to work toward improved physical and emotional health, don't expect perfection. Of course you should work hard; of course you should be disciplined; of course you should do your best. But then, when you've given it your best effort, you should be accepting of yourself, imperfect though you may be.

In heaven, we will know perfection. Here on earth, we have a few short years to wrestle with the challenges of imperfection. Let us accept these lives that God has given us—and these bodies which are ours for a brief time here on earth—with open, loving arms.

WORKING IT OUT
OBEDIENCE TO GOD IS ESSENTIAL

It's simple: When you're treating your body like a temple, you're obeying God; when you're abusing your body, you're disobeying Him.

ALWAYS GROWING IN YOUR FAITH

When it comes to your faith, God doesn't intend for you to stand still. He wants you to keep moving and growing. In fact, God's plan for you includes a lifetime of prayer, praise, and spiritual growth.

As a Christian, you should continue to grow in the love and the knowledge of your Savior as long as you live. How? By studying God's Word every day, by obeying His commandments, and by allowing His Son to reign over your heart, that's how.

Are you a woman who is continually seeking to become a more mature believer? Hopefully so, because that's exactly what you owe to yourself and to God . . . but not necessarily in that order.

STRENGTHENING YOUR FAITH
SPIRITUAL GROWTH IS ALWAYS POSSIBLE

How do you know if you can still keep growing as a Christian? Check your pulse. If it's still beating, then you can still keep growing.

MORE FROM GOD'S WORD ABOUT
TRUSTING GOD

Lord, I turn my hope to You. My God, I trust in You. Do not let me be disgraced; do not let my enemies gloat over me.

Psalm 25:1-2 HCSB

He granted their request because they trusted in Him.

1 Chronicles 5:20 HCSB

The one who understands a matter finds success, and the one who trusts in the Lord will be happy.

Proverbs 16:20 HCSB

The fear of man is a snare, but the one who trusts in the Lord is protected.

Proverbs 29:25 HCSB

Those who trust in the Lord are like Mount Zion. It cannot be shaken; it remains forever.

Psalm 125:1 HCSB

NOTES TO YOURSELF

In the space below, write down at least three things you can do this week to improve the state of your spiritual health.

_____

_____

_____

_____

_____

_____

_____

_____

_____

_____

_____

_____

_____

PERSPECTIVE AND BALANCE

*Come to Me, all you who labor and are heavy laden,
and I will give you rest. Take My yoke upon you
and learn from Me, for I am gentle and lowly in heart,
and you will find rest for your souls.
For My yoke is easy and My burden is light.*

—

Matthew 11:28-30 NKJV

THE BIBLICAL PRINCIPLE

Life is a balancing act.
To improve your balance, you should consult
your Heavenly Father many times each day.

Sometimes, amid the demands of daily life, we lose perspective. Life seems out of balance, and the pressures of everyday living seem overwhelming. What's needed is a fresh perspective, a restored sense of balance . . . and God.

If a temporary loss of perspective has robbed you of the spiritual fitness that should be yours in Christ, it's time to readjust your thought patterns. Negative thoughts are habit-forming; thankfully, so are positive ones. With practice, you can form the habit of focusing on God's priorities and your possibilities. When you do, you'll soon discover that you will spend less time fretting about your challenges and more time praising God for His gifts.

When you call upon the Lord and prayerfully seek His will, He will give you wisdom and perspective. When you make God's priorities your priorities, He will direct your steps and calm your fears. So today and every day hereafter, pray for a sense of balance and perspective. And remember: your thoughts are intensely powerful things, so handle them with care.

Some of us would do more for the Lord
if we did less.

———

Vance Havner

MORE FROM GOD'S WORD

Fix your thoughts on what is true and honorable and right. Think about things that are pure and lovely and admirable. Think about things that are excellent and worthy of praise.

Philippians 4:8 NLT

It is better to get wisdom than gold, and to choose understanding rather than silver!

Proverbs 16:16 NCV

It's better to be wise than strong.

Proverbs 24:5 MSG

People's thoughts can be like a deep well, but someone with understanding can find the wisdom there.

Proverbs 20:5 NCV

Don't copy the behavior and customs of this world, but let God transform you into a new person by changing the way you think. Then you will know what God wants you to do, and you will know how good and pleasing and perfect his will really is.

Romans 12:2 NLT

MORE THOUGHTS ABOUT BALANCE

Prescription for a happier and healthier life: resolve to slow down your pace; learn to say no gracefully; resist the temptation to chase after more pleasure, more hobbies, and more social entanglements.

James Dobson

Work is not always required of a man. There is such a thing as sacred idleness, the cultivation of which is now fearfully neglected.

George MacDonald

Jesus gives us the ultimate rest, the confidence we need, to escape the frustration and chaos of the world around us.

Billy Graham

FOOD FOR THOUGHT
IT'S UP TO YOU

Simply put, it's up to you to assume the ultimate responsibility for your health. So if you're fighting the battle of the bulge (the bulging waistline, that is), don't waste your time blaming the fast-food industry—or anybody else, for that matter. It's your body, and it's your responsibility to take care of it.

FINDING TIME FOR RECREATION

Are you one of those women who seldom takes a day off? Are you a seven-day-a-week worker bee, or a closet workaholic? If so, it's time to reorder your priorities. Why? Because an essential element of physical, emotional, and spiritual fitness is simply this: the ability to relax and enjoy leisure time.

The familiar words of Psalm 118:24 remind us of a profound yet simple truth: "This is the day the LORD has made; let us rejoice and be glad in it" (NIV). Yet we may find ourselves so wrapped up in the demands of everyday living that we forget to celebrate God's glorious gift. That's a BIG mistake.

Are you willing to relax long enough so that you can celebrate this glorious day with your family and friends? Hopefully so, because this day is a one-of-a-kind treasure that can—and should—be a cause for joyful celebration. Part of that celebration means finding an appropriate balance between work and play.

PEACE AND RENEWAL

One aspect of spiritual health is the ability to partake in the peace that only God can give. Are you willing to accept God's peace? If you can genuinely answer that question with a resounding yes, then you are richly blessed. But if you have not yet discovered "the peace that passes all understanding," today is a wonderful day to find it.

The beautiful words of John 14:27 give us hope: "Peace I leave with you, my peace I give to you . . . ." Jesus offers us peace, not as the world gives, but as He alone gives. We, as believers, can accept His peace or ignore it.

When we accept the peace of Jesus Christ into our hearts, our lives are transformed. And then, because we possess the gift of peace, we can share that gift with fellow Christians, family members, friends, and associates. If, on the other hand, we choose to ignore the gift of peace—for whatever reason—we simply cannot share what we do not possess.

Today, as a gift to yourself, to your family, and to your friends, make peace with the past by forgiving those who have harmed you. Then, claim the inner peace that is your spiritual birthright: the peace of Jesus Christ. It is offered freely; it has been paid for in full; it is yours for the asking. So ask. And then share.

WORKING IT OUT
LITTLE DECISIONS ADD UP

When taken together over a long period of time, little decisions can have big consequences. So remember: when it comes to matters of health and fitness, there are no "small" decisions.

STRENGTHENING YOUR FAITH
SPEND TIME EVERY DAY WITH GOD

Need balance? Have a daily planning session with God. A regularly scheduled time of prayer, Bible reading, and meditation can help you prioritize your day and your life. And what if you're simply too busy to spend five or ten minutes with God? If so, it's time to reorder your priorities.

MORE FROM GOD'S WORD ABOUT
GOD'S FAITHFULNESS

I will sing of the tender mercies of the Lord forever! Young and old will hear of your faithfulness. Your unfailing love will last forever. Your faithfulness is as enduring as the heavens.

Psalm 89:1-2 NLT

Because of the LORD'S great love we are not consumed, for his compassions never fail. They are new every morning; great is your faithfulness.

Lamentations 3:22-23 NIV

For the Lord is good. His unfailing love continues forever, and his faithfulness continues to each generation.

Psalm 100:5 NLT

Blessed is he whose help is the God of Jacob, whose hope is in the LORD his God, the Maker of heaven and earth, the sea, and everything in them—the LORD, who remains faithful forever.

Psalm 146:5-6 NIV

NOTES TO YOURSELF

In the space below, write down at least three things you can do to bring more peace into your life.

_____

_____

_____

_____

_____

_____

_____

_____

_____

_____

_____

_____

_____

_____

_____

_____

RECHARGING YOUR SPIRITUAL BATTERIES

Those who hope in the LORD will renew their strength.
They will soar on wings like eagles;
they will run and not grow weary,
they will walk and not be faint.

—

Isaiah 40:31 NIV

THE BIBLICAL PRINCIPLE

For the journey through life, you need energy.
The best source of energy, of course, is God.
So if you're wise, you'll ask the Creator
to energize you and guide you today and every day.

As you make the journey toward improved fitness, you'll undoubtedly run out of energy from time to time. When it happens, you can turn to God for strength and for guidance.

Andrew Murray observed, "Where there is much prayer, there will be much of the Spirit; where there is much of the Spirit, there will be ever-increasing power." These words remind us that the ultimate source of our strength is God. When we turn to Him—for guidance, for enlightenment, and for strength—we will not be disappointed.

Are you feeling exhausted? Are your emotions on edge? If so, it's time to turn things over to God in prayer. Are you weak or worried? Take the time—or, more accurately, make the time—to delve deeply into God's Holy Word. Are you spiritually depleted? Call upon fellow believers to support you, and call upon Christ to renew your spirit and your life. When you do, you'll discover that the Creator of the universe has the power to make all things new . . . including you.

Never be lacking in zeal,
but keep your spiritual fervor, serving the Lord.

—

Romans 12:11 NIV

MORE FROM GOD'S WORD

But Jesus looked at them and said, "With men this is impossible, but with God all things are possible."

Matthew 19:26 HCSB

You are the God who works wonders; You revealed Your strength among the peoples.

Psalm 77:14 HCSB

Proclaim the power of God, whose majesty is over Israel, whose power is in the skies. You are awesome, O God, in your sanctuary; the God of Israel gives power and strength to his people. Praise be to God!

Psalm 68:34-35 NIV

FOOD FOR THOUGHT
FINDING THE ENERGY TO DO GOD'S WORK

It takes energy to do God's work. And a well-rested Christian can be a much more effective worker for God. So plan your life, and your sleep, accordingly.

MORE THOUGHTS ABOUT
RENEWAL

Jesus taught us by example to get out of the rat race and recharge our batteries.

Barbara Johnson

Troubles we bear trustfully can bring us a fresh vision of God and a new outlook on life, an outlook of peace and hope.

Billy Graham

Repentance removes old sins and wrong attitudes, and it opens the way for the Holy Spirit to restore our spiritual health.

Shirley Dobson

Hope can give us life. It can provide energy that would otherwise do us in completely if we tried to operate in our own strength.

Barbara Johnson

He is the God of wholeness and restoration.

Stormie Omartian

BEWARE OF RESTAURANT FARE

In the good old days, dining out used to be an occasional treat for most families. Now, it's more of an everyday occurrence. But there's a catch: most restaurants aim for taste first, price second, and health a distant third. But you should think health first. So the next time you head out for a burger, a bagel, or any other fast food, take a minute to read the fine print that's usually posted on the wall. You may find out that the healthy-sounding treat is actually a calorie-bomb in disguise.

WORKING IT OUT
MORE EXERCISE EQUALS LESS STRESS

As exercise increases, stress usually decreases. So, if you want less stress in your life, you should exercise more frequently.

YOUR ENERGY AND GOD'S PROMISES

All of us have moments when we feel exhausted. All of us suffer through tough times, difficult days, and perplexing periods of our lives. Thankfully, God promises to give us comfort and strength if we turn to Him.

If you're a person with too many demands and too few hours in which to meet them, it's probably time to examine your priorities while you pare down your daily to-do list. While you're at it, take time to focus upon God and His love for you. Then, ask Him for the wisdom to prioritize your life and the strength to fulfill your responsibilities. God will give you the energy to do the most important things on today's to-do list if you ask Him. So ask Him . . . today.

STRENGTHENING YOUR FAITH
ENERGY DIRECTLY FROM THE SOURCE

Feeling exhausted? Try this: Start getting more sleep each night; begin a program of regular, sensible exercise; avoid harmful food and drink; and turn your problems over to God. And, the greatest of these is "turn your problems over to God."

MORE FROM GOD'S WORD ABOUT
BIBLE STUDY

All Scripture is inspired by God and is profitable for teaching, for rebuking, for correcting, for training in righteousness, so that the man of God may be complete, equipped for every good work.

2 Timothy 3:16-17 HCSB

Man shall not live by bread alone, but by every word that proceeds from the mouth of God.

Matthew 4:4 NKJV

Heaven and earth will pass away, but My words will never pass away.

Matthew 24:35 HCSB

For the word of God is living and effective and sharper than any two-edged sword, penetrating as far as to divide soul, spirit, joints, and marrow; it is a judge of the ideas and thoughts of the heart.

Hebrews 4:12 HCSB

For I am not ashamed of the gospel, because it is God's power for salvation to everyone who believes.

Romans 1:16 HCSB

NOTES TO YOURSELF

In the space below, make notes about the strength that can be yours when you follow God's path and trust His promises.

_____

_____

_____

_____

_____

_____

_____

_____

_____

_____

_____

_____

_____

MAKING GOD'S PRIORITIES YOUR PRIORITIES

Draw near to God, and He will draw near to you.

—

James 4:8 HCSB

THE BIBLICAL PRINCIPLE

Your Heavenly Father wants you to prioritize
your day and your life. And the best place to start
is by putting God first.

Have you fervently asked God to help prioritize your life? Have you asked Him for guidance and for the courage to do the things that you know need to be done? And, have you asked Him to lead you to a place of spiritual abundance and physical health? If so, then you're continually inviting your Creator to reveal Himself in a variety of ways. As a follower of Christ, you must do no less.

When you make God's priorities your priorities, you will receive God's abundance and His peace. When you make God a full partner in every aspect of your life, He will help you keep things in balance. When you allow God to reign over your heart, He will honor you with spiritual blessings that are simply too numerous to count. So, as you plan for the day ahead, make God's will your ultimate priority. When you do, every other priority will have a tendency to fall neatly into place.

Whatever you love most, be it sports, pleasure, business or God, that is your god.

—

Billy Graham

MORE FROM GOD'S WORD

Don't abandon wisdom, and she will watch over you; love her, and she will guard you.

Proverbs 4:6 HCSB

And I pray this: that your love will keep on growing in knowledge and every kind of discernment, so that you can determine what really matters and can be pure and blameless in the day of Christ.

Philippians 1:9 HCSB

So teach us to number our days, that we may gain a heart of wisdom.

Psalm 90:12 NKJV

He said to them all, "If anyone desires to come after Me, let him deny himself, and take up his cross daily, and follow Me. For whoever desires to save his life will lose it, but whoever loses his life for My sake will save it."

Luke 9:23-24 NKJV

MORE THOUGHTS ABOUT PRIORITIES

Blessed are those who know what on earth they are here on earth to do and set themselves about the business of doing it.

Max Lucado

The essence of the Christian life is Jesus: that in all things He might have the preeminence, not that in some things He might have a place.

Franklin Graham

How important it is for us—young and old—to live as if Jesus would return any day—to set our goals, make our choices, raise our children, and conduct business with the perspective of the imminent return of our Lord.

Gloria Gaither

Often our lives are strangled by things that don't ultimately matter.

Grady Nutt

NOTES TO YOURSELF

In the space below, make a few notes about your most important priorities.

LIFETIME LEARNING

The wise person makes learning a joy;
fools spout only foolishness.

—

Proverbs 15:2 NLT

THE BIBLICAL PRINCIPLE

God still has important lessons to teach you.
Your task is to be open to His instruction.

Whether you're twenty-two or a hundred and two, you've still got lots to learn. Even if you're very wise, God isn't finished with you yet, and He isn't finished teaching you important lessons about life here on earth and life eternal.

God does not intend for you to be a stagnant believer. Far from it! God wants you to continue growing as a person and as a Christian every day that you live. And make no mistake: both spiritual and intellectual growth are possible during every stage of life.

When it comes to learning life's lessons, we can either do things the easy way or the hard way. The easy way can be summed up as follows: when God teaches us a lesson, we learn it . . . the first time! Unfortunately, too many of us learn much more slowly than that.

When we resist God's instruction, He continues to teach, whether we like it or not. And if we keep making the same old mistakes, God responds by rewarding us with the same old results.

Our challenge, then, is to discern God's lessons from the experiences of everyday life. Hopefully, we learn those lessons sooner rather than later because the sooner we do, the sooner He can move on to the next lesson and the next, and the next . . .

MORE FROM GOD'S WORD

A wise person pays attention to correction that will improve his life.

Proverbs 15:31 ICB

Remember what you are taught, and listen carefully to words of knowledge.

Proverbs 23:12 NCV

The fear of the Lord is the beginning of knowledge, but fools despise wisdom and discipline.

Proverbs 1:7 NIV

The knowledge of the secrets of the kingdom of heaven has been given to you . . . .

Matthew 13:11 NIV

It is not good to have zeal without knowledge, nor to be hasty and miss the way.

Proverbs 19:2 NIV

MORE THOUGHTS ABOUT
LIFETIME LEARNING

True learning can take place at every age of life, and it doesn't have to be in the curriculum plan.

Suzanne Dale Ezell

While chastening is always difficult, if we look to God for the lesson we should learn, we will see spiritual fruit.

Vonette Bright

The wonderful thing about God's schoolroom is that we get to grade our own papers. You see, He doesn't test us so He can learn how well we're doing. He tests us so we can discover how well we're doing.

Charles Swindoll

The wise man gives proper appreciation in his life to his past. He learns to sift the sawdust of heritage in order to find the nuggets that make the current moment have any meaning.

Grady Nutt

The more wisdom enters our hearts, the more we will be able to trust our hearts in difficult situations.

John Eldredge

NOTES TO YOURSELF

In the space below, make a few notes about the lessons
that you believe God is trying to teach you today.

_____

_____

_____

_____

_____

_____

_____

_____

_____

_____

_____

_____

_____

_____

_____

_____

GOD'S PLAN FOR YOUR HEALTH

Who are those who fear the Lord? He will show them the path they should choose. They will live in prosperity, and their children will inherit the Promised Land.

—

Psalm 25:12-13 NLT

THE BIBLICAL PRINCIPLE

God has a plan for your spiritual, physical, and emotional health.

The journey toward improved health is not only a common-sense exercise in personal discipline, it is also a spiritual journey ordained by our Creator. God does not intend that we abuse our bodies by giving in to excessive appetites or to slothful behavior. To the contrary, God has instructed us to protect our physical bodies to the greatest extent we can. To do otherwise is to disobey Him.

When you make the decision to seek God's will for your life—and you should—then you will contemplate His Word, and you will be watchful for His signs. God intends to use you in wonderful, unexpected ways if you let Him. But be forewarned: the decision to seek God's plan and fulfill His purpose is ultimately a decision that you must make by yourself and for yourself. The consequences of that decision have implications that are both profound and eternal, so choose carefully. And then, as you go about your daily activities, keep your eyes and ears open, as well as your heart, because God is patiently trying to get His message through . . . and there's no better moment than this one for you to help Him.

MORE FROM GOD'S WORD

And we know that in all things God works for the good of those who love him, who have been called according to his purpose.

Romans 8:28 NIV

It is God who works in you to will and to act according to his good purpose.

Philippians 2:13 NIV

The Lord says, "I will make you wise and show you where to go. I will guide you and watch over you."

Psalm 32:8 NCV

Lord, You light my lamp; my God illuminates my darkness.

Psalm 18:28 HCSB

FOOD FOR THOUGHT
JUST SAY NO TO JUNK FOOD

We live in a junk-food society, but you shouldn't let your house become junk-food heaven. Make your home a haven of healthy foods. And remember, it's never too soon to teach your kids good habits . . . and that includes the very good habit of sensible eating.

MORE THOUGHTS ABOUT
GOD'S PLAN

With God, it's never "Plan B" or "second best." It's always "Plan A." And, if we let Him, He'll make something beautiful of our lives.

Gloria Gaither

God has a plan for the life of every Christian. Every circumstance, every turn of destiny, all things work together for your good and for His glory.

Billy Graham

When the dream of our heart is one that God has planted there, a strange happiness flows into us. At that moment, all of the spiritual resources of the universe are released to help us. Our praying is then at one with the will of God and becomes a channel for the Creator's purposes for us and our world.

Catherine Marshall

God's all-sufficiency is a major. Your inability is a minor. Major in majors, not in minors.

Corrie ten Boom

ACTIONS REFLECT BELIEFS

English clergyman Thomas Fuller observed, "He does not believe who does not live according to his beliefs." These words are most certainly true. We may proclaim our beliefs to our hearts' content, but our proclamations will mean nothing—to others or to ourselves—unless we accompany our words with deeds that match. The sermons that we live are far more compelling than the ones we preach.

Like it or not, your life is an accurate reflection of your creed. If this fact gives you some cause for concern, don't bother talking about the changes that you intend to make—make them. And then, when your good deeds speak for themselves—as they most certainly will—don't interrupt.

WORKING IT OUT
IT'S PART OF GOD'S PLAN FOR YOU

Do you think God wants you to develop healthy habits? Of course He does! Physical, emotional, and spiritual fitness are all part of God's plan for you. But it's up to you to make certain that a healthy lifestyle is a fundamental part of your plan, too.

DOING THINGS HIS WAY

D o you want to experience a life filled with abundance and peace? If so, here's a word of warning: you'll need to resist the temptation to do things "your way" and you must commit, instead, to do things God's way.

Just for the record, here are the facts: 1. God has plans for your life that are far grander than you can imagine. 2. It's up to you to discover those plans and accomplish them . . . or not.

Sometimes, God's plans are crystal clear, but other times, He may lead you through the wilderness before He delivers you to the Promised Land. So be patient, keep praying, and keep seeking His will for your life. When you do, you'll be amazed at the marvelous things that an all-powerful, all-knowing God can do.

STRENGTHENING YOUR FAITH
FOLLOW HIS LEAD

God has a plan for the world and for you. When you discover His plan for your life—and when you follow in the footsteps of His Son—you will be rewarded. The place where God is leading you is the place where you must go.

MORE FROM GOD'S WORD ABOUT
VALUES

God's Way is not a matter of mere talk; it's an empowered life.

1 Corinthians 4:20 MSG

Walk in a manner worthy of the God who calls you into His own kingdom and glory.

1 Thessalonians 2:12 NASB

Therefore, since we have this ministry, as we have received mercy, we do not give up. Instead, we have renounced shameful secret things, not walking in deceit or distorting God's message, but in God's sight we commend ourselves to every person's conscience by an open display of the truth.

2 Corinthians 4:1-2 HCSB

We must not become tired of doing good. We will receive our harvest of eternal life at the right time if we do not give up.

Galatians 6:9 NCV

Blessed are those who hunger and thirst for righteousness, because they will be filled.

Matthew 5:6 HCSB

NOTES TO YOURSELF

In the space below, write down some of the things you think God wants you to do today, this week, and this year.

_____

_____

_____

_____

_____

_____

_____

_____

_____

_____

_____

_____

_____

_____

_____

_____

_____

GETTING ENOUGH REST?

*Come to Me, all you who are weary and burdened,
and I will give you rest.*

—

Matthew 11:28-30 NKJV

THE BIBLICAL PRINCIPLE

God wants you to get enough rest.
The world wants you to burn the candle at both ends.
Trust God.

Even the most inspired Christians can, from time to time, find themselves running on empty. The demands of daily life can drain us of our strength and rob us of the joy that is rightfully ours in Christ. When we find ourselves tired, discouraged, or worse, there is a source from which we can draw the power needed to recharge our spiritual batteries. That source is God.

God intends that His children lead joyous lives filled with abundance and peace. But sometimes, abundance and peace seem very far away. It is then that we must turn to God for renewal, and when we do, He will restore us.

God expects us to work hard, but He also intends for us to rest. When we fail to take the rest that we need, we do a disservice to ourselves and to our families.

Is your spiritual battery running low? Is your energy on the wane? Are your emotions frayed? If so, it's time to turn your thoughts and your prayers to God. And when you're finished, it's time to rest.

I said to myself, "Relax and rest.
God has showered you
with blessings."

—

Psalm 116:7 MSG

FOOD FOR THOUGHT
GETTING EIGHT HOURS IS IMPORTANT

Most adults need about eight hours of sleep each night. If you're depriving yourself of much-needed sleep in order to stay up and watch late-night television, you've developed a bad habit. Instead, do yourself a favor: turn off the TV and go to bed.

MORE FROM GOD'S WORD

And be not conformed to this world: but be ye transformed by the renewing of your mind.

Romans 12:2 KJV

And the apostles gathered themselves together unto Jesus, and told him all things, both what they had done, and what they had taught. And he said unto them, Come ye yourselves apart into a desert place, and rest a while.

Mark 6:30-31 KJV

I will lift up mine eyes unto the hills, from whence cometh my help. My help cometh from the Lord, which made heaven and earth.

Psalm 121:1-2 KJV

For six days work may be done, but on the seventh day there is a sabbath of complete rest, a holy convocation. You shall not do any work; it is a sabbath to the LORD in all your dwellings.

Leviticus 23:3 NASB

MORE THOUGHTS ABOUT
GETTING ENOUGH REST

Satan does some of his worst work on exhausted Christians when nerves are frayed and their minds are faint.

Vance Havner

One reason so much American Christianity is a mile wide and an inch deep is that Christians are simply tired. Sometimes you need to kick back and rest for Jesus' sake.

Dennis Swanberg

Sleep is the golden chain that ties health and our bodies together.

Thomas Dekker

Take a rest; a field that has rested gives a bountiful crop.

Ovid

Early to bed and early to rise, makes a man healthy, wealthy, and wise.

Ben Franklin

EXHAUSTED? TRY TURNING OFF
THE TV A LITTLE EARLIER

Y ou live in a world that tempts you to stay up late—very late. But too much late-night TV, combined with too little sleep, is a prescription for exhaustion, ill health, ill temper, or all three. So do yourself, your boss, and your loved ones a big favor. Arrange your TV schedule and your life so you get eight hours of sleep every night.

Since you can't cheat Mr. Sandman, don't even try. When in doubt, do the smart thing: do whatever it takes to get the sleep you need. It's the smart way to schedule your day and your life.

WORKING IT OUT
MAKE IT FUN

If you genuinely want to exercise more, find exercise that you enjoy. And if you can't seem to find exercise that you enjoy, search for ways to make your current exercise program a little less painful and a little more fun.

IF YOU'RE HAVING TROUBLE SLEEPING, CONSIDER THE FOLLOWING TIPS

1. Reduce your intake of caffeine or eliminate caffeine entirely from your diet. The residual effects of too much coffee (or too many caffeine-loaded soft drinks) may be contributing to your sleeplessness.

2. At least one hour before bedtime, begin the process of preparing for sleep by putting yourself into a calmer state. Don't watch television programs that might upset you or "get your juices flowing." Instead, engage in quieter pursuits (such as reading) in order to ready yourself for a good night's sleep.

3. If you can't fall asleep quickly, don't lay in bed and worry about the fact that you are not sleeping. Get up, pick up a book, and read until you feel tired. Then go back to bed. Your bed should be a place for sleeping, not a place for worrying.

4. Establish regular sleep patterns by getting up at the same time every day. Even if you don't fall asleep until a very late hour, force yourself out of bed at the same time each morning. This practice will, within a few weeks, help you establish a more normal pattern of sleep.

5. Troubles and worries are always magnified during the nighttime hours. If you are too worried about a particular topic to fall asleep, do not lay in bed and obsess over the problem. Instead, get up, take pencil and paper, and write down your worries, along with an action plan to solve them.

6. Engage in sensible physical exercise on a regular basis.

7. If you or someone close to you feels that your lack of sleep is posing a hazard to your physical or emotional well-being, consult your physician.

8. Remember the words of Victor Hugo: "Have courage for all the great sorrows of life and patience for the small ones. And when you have finished your daily task, go to sleep. God is awake."

STRENGTHENING YOUR FAITH
ANGRY? MAYBE YOU'RE JUST TIRED

Oftentimes, our anger is nothing more than exhaustion in disguise. When in doubt, get eight hours of sleep.

MORE FROM GOD'S WORD ABOUT PEACE

And the peace of God, which surpasses every thought, will guard your hearts and your minds in Christ Jesus. Finally brothers, whatever is true, whatever is honorable, whatever is just, whatever is pure, whatever is lovely, whatever is commendable—if there is any moral excellence and if there is any praise—dwell on these things.

Philippians 4:7-8 HCSB

Abundant peace belongs to those who love Your instruction; nothing makes them stumble.

Psalm 119:165 HCSB

And let the peace of God rule in your hearts...and be ye thankful.

Colossians 3:15 KJV

You will keep in perfect peace him whose mind is steadfast, because he trusts in you.

Isaiah 26:3 NIV

I have told you these things so that in Me you may have peace. In the world you have suffering. But take courage! I have conquered the world.

John 16:33 HCSB

NOTES TO YOURSELF

In the space below, write down several things you can do to insure that you get enough rest each night.

_____

_____

_____

_____

_____

_____

_____

_____

_____

_____

_____

_____

_____

_____

_____

MISDIRECTED WORSHIP: THE TRAGEDY OF ADDICTION

Let us walk with decency, as in the daylight: not in carousing and drunkenness.

—

Romans 13:13 HCSB

THE BIBLICAL PRINCIPLE

You must guard your heart against addiction . . . or else.

The dictionary defines addiction as " the compulsive need for a habit-forming substance; the condition of being habitually and compulsively occupied with something." That definition is accurate, but incomplete. For Christians, addiction has an additional meaning: it means compulsively worshipping something other than God.

Ours is a highly addictive society. Why? The answer is straightforward: supply and demand. The supply of addictive substances continues to grow; the affordability and availability of these substances makes them highly attractive to consumers; and the overall demand for addictive substances has increased as more and more users have become addicted to an ever-expanding array of substances and compulsions.

You know people who are full-blown addicts—probably lots of people. If you, or someone you love, is suffering from the blight of addiction, the following ideas are worth remembering:

1. For the addict, addiction comes first. In the life of an addict, addiction rules. God, of course, commands otherwise. God says, "You shall have no other gods before Me," (Exodus 20:3 NKJV) and He means precisely what He says. Our task, as believers, is to put God in His proper place: first place.

2. You cannot cure another person's addiction, but you can encourage that person to seek help. Addicts are cured when they decide, not when you decide. What you can do is this: you can be supportive, and you can encourage the addict to find the help that he or she needs. (Luke 10:25-37)

3. If you are living with an addicted person, think about safety: yours and your family's. Addiction is life-threatening and life-shortening. Don't let someone else's addiction threaten your safety or the safety of your loved ones. (Proverbs 22:3)

4. Don't assist in prolonging the addiction: When you interfere with the negative consequences that might otherwise accompany an addict's negative behaviors, you are inadvertently "enabling" the addict to continue the destructive cycle of addiction. So don't be an enabler. (Proverbs 15:31)

5. Help is available: Lots of people have experienced addiction and lived to tell about it. They want to help. Let them. (Proverbs 27:17)

6. Cure is possible. With God's help, no addiction is incurable. And with God, no situation is hopeless. (Matthew 19:26)

Above all, we must be especially alert against the beginnings of temptation, for the enemy is more easily conquered if he is refused admittance to the mind and is met beyond the threshold when he knocks.

—

Thomas à Kempis

FOOD FOR THOUGHT
RELAPSE? PROBABLY.

If you're on a new health regimen, you may relapse back into your old, unhealthy habits. If so, don't waste time or energy beating yourself up. If you've "fallen off the wagon," simply pick yourself up, dust yourself off, and get back on it. God was with you when you were riding that wagon the first time, He was with you when you fell, and He'll welcome you back on the wagon when you're wise enough to climb back on.

MORE FROM GOD'S WORD

Do not carouse with drunkards and gluttons, for they are on their way to poverty.

Proverbs 23:20-21 NLT

Don't be drunk with wine, because that will ruin your life. Instead, let the Holy Spirit fill and control you.

Ephesians 5:18 NLT

Watch out! Don't let me find you living in careless ease and drunkenness, and filled with the worries of this life. Don't let that day catch you unaware.

Luke 21:34 NLT

Be sober! Be on the alert! Your adversary the Devil is prowling around like a roaring lion, looking for anyone he can devour.

1 Peter 5:8 HCSB

You shall have no other gods before Me.

Exodus 20:3 NKJV

MORE THOUGHTS ABOUT TEMPTATION

Temptation is not a sin. Even Jesus was tempted. The Lord Jesus gives you the strength needed to resist temptation.

Corrie ten Boom

The chains of habit are too weak to be felt until they are too strong to be broken.

Samuel Johnson

Do not fight the temptation in detail. Turn from it. Look ONLY at your Lord. Sing. Read. Work.

Amy Carmichael

If you want to form a new habit, get to work. If you want to break a bad habit, get on your knees.

Marie T. Freeman

A man may not be responsible for his last drink, but he certainly was for the first.

Billy Graham

SAFETY MATTERS

We live in a world that can be a dangerous place, especially for those who are inclined toward risky behaviors. Some risk takers are easy to spot: they jump out of little airplanes, scurry up tall mountains, or race very fast automobiles.

Most risk takers, however, are not so bold; instead, they take more subtle risks that endanger themselves, their friends, and their families. They drink and drive, or they smoke cigarettes, or they neglect to fasten their seat belts, or they engage in countless other behaviors that, while not as glamorous as mountain climbing, are equally as dangerous.

This world holds enough hazards of its own without our adding to those risks by foolishly neglecting our own personal safety and the safety of those around us. So, the next time you're tempted to do something foolish, remember that the body you're putting at risk belongs not only to you, but also to God. And He hopes that you'll behave wisely.

YOU'RE RESPONSIBLE

Remember that ultimately you and you alone are responsible for controlling your appetites. Others may warn you, help you, or encourage you, but in the end, the habits that rule your life are the very same habits that you yourself have formed. Thankfully, since you formed these habits, you can also break them—if you decide to do so.

WORKING IT OUT
SOMETIMES, YOU CAN'T DO IT ALONE

If you can't seem to get a handle on your appetites, the time to address your problem is today, not tomorrow. Gather your courage and pay a visit to your pastor, to a counselor, or to a local 12-step group. Help is waiting, but you'll need to ask for it. So ask.

STRENGTHENING YOUR FAITH
ADDICTION DESTROYS

You must guard your heart against dangerous temptations and life-sapping addictions . . . or else.

MORE FROM GOD'S WORD ABOUT
GOD'S GRACE

But God, who is abundant in mercy, because of His great love that He had for us, made us alive with the Messiah even though we were dead in trespasses. By grace you are saved!

Ephesians 2:4-5 HCSB

My grace is sufficient for you, for My strength is made perfect in weakness.

2 Corinthians 12:9 NKJV

And we have seen and testify that the Father has sent the Son as Savior of the world.

1 John 4:14 NKJV

For by grace you are saved through faith, and this is not from yourselves; it is God's gift—not from works, so that no one can boast.

Ephesians 2:8-9 HCSB

In Him we have redemption through His blood, the forgiveness of our trespasses, according to the riches of His grace that He lavished on us with all wisdom and understanding.

Ephesians 1:7-8 HCSB

NOTES TO YOURSELF

In the space below, make a short list of the unhealthy foods or drinks that are most tempting to you. Then, ask God to help you avoid them today.

_____

_____

_____

_____

_____

_____

_____

_____

_____

_____

_____

_____

_____

BE PATIENT
AND TRUST GOD

Be still before the Lord and wait patiently for Him.

—

Psalm 37:7 NIV

THE BIBLICAL PRINCIPLE

When you learn to be more patient,
you'll make your world—and your heart—
a more peaceful and less stressful place.

Psalm 37:7 commands us to wait patiently for God. But as busy women in a fast-paced world, many of us find that waiting quietly for God is difficult. Why? Because we are fallible human beings seeking to live according to our own timetables, not God's. In our better moments, we realize that patience is not only a virtue, but it is also a commandment from God.

We human beings are impatient by nature. We know what we want, and we know exactly when we want it: NOW! But, God knows better. He has created a world that unfolds according to His plans, not our own. As believers, we must trust His wisdom and His goodness.

God instructs us to be patient in all things. We must be patient with our families, our friends, our associates, and ourselves. We must also be patient with our Creator as He unfolds His plan for our lives. And that's as it should be. After all, think how patient God has been with us.

Patience is the companion of wisdom.

—

St. Augustine

MORE FROM GOD'S WORD

Rejoice in hope; be patient in affliction; be persistent in prayer.
Romans 12:12 HCSB

Now we exhort you, brethren, warn those who are unruly, comfort the fainthearted, uphold the weak, be patient with all.
1 Thessalonians 5:14 NKJV

Be gentle to everyone, able to teach, and patient.
2 Timothy 2:23 HCSB

Love is patient; love is kind.
1 Corinthians 13:4 HCSB

A patient spirit is better than a proud spirit.
Ecclesiastes 7:8 HCSB

200

MORE THOUGHTS ABOUT
PATIENCE

Wisdom always waits for the right time to act, while emotion always pushes for action right now.

Joyce Meyer

How do you wait upon the Lord? First you must learn to sit at His feet and take time to listen to His words.

Kay Arthur

Let me encourage you to continue to wait with faith. God may not perform a miracle, but He is trustworthy to touch you and make you whole where there used to be a hole.

Lisa Whelchel

Waiting is the hardest kind of work, but God knows best, and we may joyfully leave all in His hands.

Lottie Moon

We must learn to wait. There is grace supplied to the one who waits.

Mrs. Charles E. Cowman

NOTES TO YOURSELF

In the space below, make notes about some specific things you can do to become a more patient person.

_____

_____

_____

_____

_____

_____

_____

_____

_____

_____

_____

_____

_____

_____

_____

_____

THE POWER OF DAILY WORSHIP AND MEDITATION

Man shall not live by bread alone,
but by every word that proceeds from the mouth of God.

—

Matthew 4:4 NKJV

THE BIBLICAL PRINCIPLE

God's Word has the power to change
every aspect of your life,
including your health.

Are you concerned about your spiritual, physical, or emotional fitness? If so, there is a timeless source of advice and comfort upon which you can—and should—depend. That source is the Holy Bible.

God's Word has much to say about every aspect of your life, including your health. If you face personal health challenges that seem almost insoluble, have faith and seek God's wisdom. If you can't seem to get yourself on a sensible diet or on a program of regular physical exercise, consult God's teachings. If your approach to your physical or emotional health has, up to this point, been undisciplined, pray for the strength to do what you know is right.

God has given you the Holy Bible for the purpose of knowing His promises, His power, His commandments, His wisdom, His love, and His Son. As you seek to improve the state of your own health, study God's teachings and apply them to your life. When you do, you will be blessed, now and forever.

A life lived without reflection can be
very superficial and empty.

—

Elisabeth Elliot

MORE FROM GOD'S WORD

He awakens Me morning by morning, He awakens My ear to hear as the learned. The Lord God has opened My ear.

Isaiah 50:4-5 NKJV

Lord, You are my lamp; the Lord illuminates my darkness.

2 Samuel 22:29 HCSB

Teach me Your way, Lord, and I will live by Your truth. Give me an undivided mind to fear Your name.

Psalm 86:11 HCSB

I will instruct you and show you the way to go; with My eye on you, I will give counsel.

Psalm 32:8 HCSB

FOOD FOR THOUGHT
WHAT IS YOUR REFRIGERATOR
TRYING TO TELL YOU?

Take a careful look inside your refrigerator. Are the contents reflective of a healthy lifestyle? And if your fridge is overflowing with junk foods, it's time to rethink your shopping habits.

MORE THOUGHTS ABOUT
YOUR DAILY DEVOTIONAL

How motivating it has been for me to view my early morning devotions as time of retreat alone with Jesus, Who desires that I "come with Him by myself to a quiet place" in order to pray, read His Word, listen for His voice, and be renewed in my spirit.

Anne Graham Lotz

Every day has its own particular brand of holiness to discover and worship appropriately.

Annie Dillard

God is a place of safety you can run to, but it helps if you are running to Him on a daily basis so that you are in familiar territory.

Stormie Omartian

I suggest you discipline yourself to spend time daily in a systematic reading of God's Word. Make this "quiet time" a priority that nobody can change.

Warren Wiersbe

A person with no devotional life generally struggles with faith and obedience.

Charles Stanley

YOUR FITNESS AND YOUR FAITH

Faith and fitness. These two words may seem disconnected, but they are not. If you're about to begin a regimen of vigorous physical exercise, then you will find it helpful to begin a regimen of vigorous spiritual exercise, too. Why? Because the physical, emotional, and spiritual aspects of your life are interconnected. In other words, you cannot "compartmentalize" physical fitness in one category of your being and spiritual fitness in another—every facet of your life has an impact on the person you are today and the person you will become tomorrow. That's why your body is so important to God—your body is, quite literally, the "temple" that houses "the Spirit of God" that dwells within you (1 Corinthians 3:16).

God's Word contains powerful lessons about every aspect of your life, including your health. So, if you're concerned about your spiritual, physical, or emotional health, the first place to turn is that timeless source of comfort and assurance, the Holy Bible. When you open your Bible and begin reading, you'll quickly be reminded of this fact: when you face concerns of any sort—including health-related challenges—God is with you. And His healing touch, like His love, endures forever.

God has given us the Bible for the purpose of knowing His promises, His power, His commandments, His wisdom, His love, and His Son. As we study God's teachings and apply them to our lives, we live by the Word that shall never pass away. So if you're about to begin a new fitness program, be sure that you also pay careful attention to God's program by studying His Word every day of your life.

WORKING IT OUT
WHAT THE BIBLE SAYS ABOUT
YOUR HEALTH

God's Word is full of advice about health, moderation, and sensible living. When you come across these passages, take them to heart and put them to use.

SPENDING QUIET TIME WITH GOD

The Bible promises that a good way to know God is to be still and listen to Him. But sometimes, you may find it hard to slow down and listen. As the demands of everyday life weigh down upon you, you may become so wrapped up in your obligations that you just don't take enough time for God. A far better strategy, of course, is to quiet yourself every day. When you do, you will experience the Father's presence and His love. Then, God will touch your heart, He will restore your spirits, and He will give you the perspective you need to make good decisions.

As you petition God each morning, ask Him for the strength and the wisdom to live moderately and wisely. Ask Him to help you treat your body as His temple. During the day ahead, you will face countless temptations to do otherwise, but with God's help, you can treat your body as the priceless, one-of-a-kind gift that it most certainly is.

STRENGTHENING YOUR FAITH
STUDYING THE BIBLE IS NOT ENOUGH

Your daily devotional should have a major impact on your day. Don't just study the Bible; live by it!

MORE FROM GOD'S WORD ABOUT SILENCE

Be still, and know that I am God.

Psalm 46:10 NKJV

Be silent before the Lord and wait expectantly for Him.

Psalm 37:7 HCSB

In quietness and confidence shall be your strength.

Isaiah 30:15 NKJV

I am not alone, because the Father is with Me.

John 16:32 HCSB

Draw near to God, and He will draw near to you.

James 4:8 HCSB

NOTES TO YOURSELF

In the space below, write down some of the benefits that you earn whenever you start your day with God.

_____

_____

_____

_____

_____

_____

_____

_____

_____

_____

_____

_____

_____

_____

_____

_____

PUTTING FAITH ABOVE FEELINGS

Now the just shall live by faith.

—

Hebrews 10:38 NKJV

THE BIBLICAL PRINCIPLE

God's love is real; His peace is real; His support is real.
And, you must never let your emotions
obscure these facts.

Who is in charge of your emotions? Is it you, or have you formed the unfortunate habit of letting other people—or troubling situations—determine the quality of your thoughts and the direction of your day? If you're wise—and if you'd like to build a better life for yourself and your loved ones—you'll learn to control your emotions before your emotions control you.

Human emotions are highly variable, decidedly unpredictable, and often unreliable. Our emotions are like the weather, only far more fickle. So we must learn to live by faith, not by the ups and downs of our own emotional roller coasters.

Sometime during this day, you will probably be gripped by a strong negative feeling. Distrust it. Reign it in. Test it. And turn it over to God. Your emotions will inevitably change; God will not. So trust Him completely as you watch those negative feelings slowly evaporate into thin air—which, of course, they will.

Emotions we have not poured out in the safe hands
of God can turn into feelings of hopelessness
and depression. God is safe.

—

Beth Moore

MORE FROM GOD'S WORD

All bitterness, anger and wrath, insult and slander must be removed from you, along with all wickedness. And be kind and compassionate to one another, forgiving one another, just as God also forgave you in Christ.

Ephesians 4:31-32 HCSB

A patient person [shows] great understanding, but a quick-tempered one promotes foolishness.

Proverbs 14:29 HCSB

Everyone must be quick to hear, slow to speak, and slow to anger, for man's anger does not accomplish God's righteousness.

James 1:19-20 HCSB

For this very reason, make every effort to supplement your faith with goodness, goodness with knowledge, knowledge with self-control, self-control with endurance, endurance with godliness.

2 Peter 1:5-6 HCSB

But now you must also put away all the following: anger, wrath, malice, slander, and filthy language from your mouth.

Colossians 3:8 HCSB

MORE THOUGHTS ABOUT EMOTIONS

The only serious mistake we can make is the mistake that Psalm 121 prevents: the mistake of supposing that God's interest in us waxes and wanes in response to our spiritual temperature.

Eugene Peterson

I may no longer depend on pleasant impulses to bring me before the Lord. I must rather respond to principles I know to be right, whether I feel them to be enjoyable or not.

Jim Elliot

Our feelings do not affect God's facts. They may blow up, like clouds, and cover the eternal things that we do most truly believe. We may not see the shining of the promises—but they still shine! His strength is not for one moment less because of our human weakness.

Amy Carmichael

If you want to receive emotional healing from God and come into an area of wholeness, you must realize that healing is a process, and you must allow the Lord to deal with you and your problem in His own way and in His own time.

Joyce Meyer

NOTES TO YOURSELF

In the space below, make notes about the rewards that are yours whenever you are able to control negative emotions.

YOU'RE ACCOUNTABLE

But each person should examine his own work,
and then he will have a reason for boasting in himself alone,
and not in respect to someone else.
For each person will have to carry his own load.

—

Galatians 6:4-5 HCSB

THE BIBLICAL PRINCIPLE

If you want to establish a healthy lifestyle,
you need to assume responsibility
for your actions.
Once you begin to hold yourself accountable,
you'll begin to grow emotionally
and spiritually.

We humans are masters at passing the buck. Why? Because passing the buck is easier than fixing, and criticizing others is so much easier than improving ourselves. So instead of solving our problems legitimately (by doing the work required to solve them) we are inclined to fret, to blame, and to criticize, while doing precious little else. When we do, our problems, quite predictably, remain unsolved.

Whether you like it or not, you (and only you) are accountable for your actions. But because you are human, you'll be sorely tempted to pass the blame. Avoid that temptation at all costs.

Problem-solving builds character. Every time you straighten your back and resist temptation, you'll strengthen not only your backbone but also your spirit. So, instead of looking for someone to blame, look for something to improve (beginning with yourself), and then get busy improving it. And, as you consider your own situation, remember this: God has a way of helping those who help themselves, but He doesn't spend much time helping those who don't.

The Bible teaches that we are accountable
to one another for our conduct and character.

—

Charles Stanley

MORE FROM GOD'S WORD

Therefore as you have received Christ Jesus the Lord, walk in Him.

Colossians 2:6 HCSB

Don't be deceived: God is not mocked. For whatever a man sows he will also reap, because the one who sows to his flesh will reap corruption from the flesh, but the one who sows to the Spirit will reap eternal life from the Spirit.

Galatians 6:7-8 HCSB

Who is wise and understanding among you? He should show his works by good conduct with wisdom's gentleness.

James 3:13 HCSB

Even a young man is known by his actions—by whether his behavior is pure and upright.

Proverbs 20:11 HCSB

Lead a tranquil and quiet life in all godliness and dignity.

1 Timothy 2:2 HCSB

MORE THOUGHTS ABOUT
ACCOUNTABILITY

Generally speaking, accountability is a willingness to share our activities, conduct, and fulfillment of assigned responsibilities with others.

Charles Stanley

Though I know intellectually how vulnerable I am to pride and power, I am the last one to know when I succumb to their seduction. That's why spiritual Lone Rangers are so dangerous—and why we must depend on trusted brothers and sisters who love us enough to tell us the truth.

Chuck Colson

We urgently need people who encourage and inspire us to move toward God and away from the world's enticing pleasures.

Jim Cymbala

Although God causes all things to work together for good for His children, He still holds us accountable for our behavior.

Kay Arthur

NOTES TO YOURSELF

In the space below, write about one specific area of responsibility that is uniquely yours, and think about a specific step you can take today to better fulfill that responsibility.

_____

_____

_____

_____

_____

_____

_____

_____

_____

_____

_____

_____

_____

_____

_____

FITNESS IS A FORM OF WORSHIP

Worship the Lord your God and . . . serve Him only.

—

Matthew 4:10 HCSB

THE BIBLICAL PRINCIPLE

When you worship God with a sincere heart,
He will guide your steps and bless your life.

What does worship have to do with fitness? That depends on how you define worship. If you consider worship to be a "Sunday-only" activity, an activity that occurs only inside the four walls of your local church, then fitness and worship may seem totally unrelated. But, if you view worship as an activity that impacts every facet of your life—if you consider worship to be something far more than a "one-day-a-week" obligation—then you understand that every aspect of your life is a form of worship. And that includes keeping your body physically fit.

Make no mistake: All of mankind (including you) is engaged in worship...of one kind or another. The question is not whether we worship, but what we worship. Some of us choose to worship our Heavenly Father. The result is a plentiful harvest of joy, peace, and abundance. Others distance themselves from God by placing the desire for personal gratification above the need for spiritual gratification. To do so can be a terrible mistake with eternal consequences.

Every day provides opportunities to put God where He belongs: at the center of our lives. When we do so, we worship not just with our words, but also with our deeds. And one way that we can honor our Heavenly Father is by treating our bodies with care and respect.

The Bible makes it clear: "Your body is the temple of the Holy Spirit" (1 Corinthians 6:19 NLT). Treat it that way. And consider your fitness regimen to be one way—a very important way—of worshipping God.

FOOD FOR THOUGHT
DON'T FOCUS ON FOOD;
FOCUS ON GOD

Don't worship food. Honor the body that God gave you by eating sensible portions of sensible foods.

MORE FROM GOD'S WORD

Worship the Lord with gladness. Come before him, singing with joy. Acknowledge that the Lord is God! He made us, and we are his. We are his people, the sheep of his pasture.

Psalm 100:2-3 NLT

A time is coming and has now come when the true worshipers will worship the Father in spirit and truth, for they are the kind of worshipers the Father seeks. God is spirit, and his worshipers must worship in spirit and in truth.

John 4:23-24 NIV

I rejoiced with those who said to me, "Let us go to the house of the Lord."

Psalm 122:1 HCSB

And every day they devoted themselves to meeting together in the temple complex, and broke bread from house to house. They ate their food with gladness and simplicity of heart, praising God and having favor with all the people. And every day the Lord added those being saved to them.

Acts 2:46-47 HCSB

MORE THOUGHTS ABOUT WORSHIP

It's the definition of worship: A hungry heart finding the Father's feast. A searching soul finding the Father's face. A wandering pilgrim spotting the Father's house. Finding God. Finding God seeking us. This is worship. This is a worshiper.

Max Lucado

Spiritual worship is focusing all we are on all He is.

Beth Moore

To worship Him in truth means to worship Him honestly, without hypocrisy, standing open and transparent before Him.

Anne Graham Lotz

God asks that we worship Him with our concentrated minds as well as with our wills and emotions. A divided and scattered mind is not effective.

Catherine Marshall

Worship is your spirit responding to God's Spirit.

Rick Warren

REMEMBER THE SABBATH

When God gave Moses the Ten Commandments, it became perfectly clear that our Heavenly Father intends for us to make the Sabbath a holy day, a day for worship, for contemplation, for fellowship, and for rest. Yet we live in a seven-day-a-week world, a world that all too often treats Sunday as a regular workday.

One way to strengthen your faith is by giving God at least one day each week. If you carve out the time for a day of worship and praise, you'll be amazed at the impact it will have on the rest of your week. But if you fail to honor God's day, if you treat the Sabbath as a day to work or a day to party, you'll miss out on a harvest of blessings that is only available one day each week.

How does your family observe the Lord's day? When church is over, do you treat Sunday like any other day of the week? If so, it's time to think long and hard about your family's schedule and your family's priorities. And if you've been treating Sunday as just another day, it's time to break that habit. When Sunday rolls around, don't try to fill every spare moment. Take time to rest . . . Father's orders!

It is impossible to worship God
and remain unchanged.

—

Henry Blackaby

WORKING IT OUT
CONSIDER YOUR HEALTHY LIFESTYLE
A FORM OF WORSHIP

When God described your body as a temple, He wasn't
kidding. Show your respect for God's Word by keeping
your temple in tip-top shape.

PRAISE HIM

When is the best time to praise God? In church? Before dinner is served? When we tuck little children into bed? None of the above. The best time to praise God is all day, every day, to the greatest extent we can, with thanksgiving in our hearts.

Too many of us, even well-intentioned believers, tend to "compartmentalize" our waking hours into a few familiar categories: work, rest, play, family time, and worship. To do so is a mistake. Worship and praise should be woven into the fabric of everything we do; it should never be relegated to a weekly three-hour visit to church on Sunday morning.

Mrs. Charles E. Cowman, the author of the classic devotional text, *Streams in the Desert*, wrote, "Two wings are necessary to lift our souls toward God: prayer and praise. Prayer asks. Praise accepts the answer." Today, find a little more time to lift your concerns to God in prayer, and praise Him for all that He has done. He's listening . . . and He wants to hear from you.

MORE FROM GOD'S WORD ABOUT PRAISE AND THANKSGIVING

It is good to give thanks to the Lord, and to sing praises to Your name, O Most High.

Psalm 92:1 NKJV

And let the peace of the Messiah, to which you were also called in one body, control your hearts. Be thankful.

Colossians 3:15 HCSB

Therefore as you have received Christ Jesus the Lord, walk in Him, rooted and built up in Him and established in the faith, just as you were taught, and overflowing with thankfulness.

Colossians 2:6-7 HCSB

In everything give thanks; for this is the will of God in Christ Jesus for you.

1 Thessalonians 5:18 NKJV

STRENGTHENING YOUR FAITH
NOT JUST SUNDAY MORNING

Worship is not meant to be boxed up in a church building on Sunday morning. To the contrary, praise and worship should be woven into the very fabric of our lives.

NOTES TO YOURSELF

In the space below, make notes about specific ways that you can worship God seven days a week.

DAY 30

YOUR PHYSICAL AND SPIRITUAL FITNESS: WHO'S IN CHARGE?

But seek ye first the kingdom of God, and his righteousness; and all these things shall be added unto you.

Matthew 6:33 KJV

THE BIBLICAL PRINCIPLE

God deserves first place in your life . . .
and you deserve the experience
of putting Him there.

One of the surest ways to improve your health and your life—and the best way—is to do it with God as your partner. When you put God first in every aspect of your life, you'll be comforted by the knowledge that His wisdom is the ultimate wisdom and that His plans are the right plans for you. When you put God first, your outlook will change, your priorities will change, your behaviors will change, and your health will change. When you put Him first, you'll experience the genuine peace and lasting comfort that only He can give.

In the book of Exodus, God instructs us to place no gods before Him (20:3). Does God rule your heart? Make certain that the honest answer to this question is a resounding yes. And then prepare yourself for the cascade of spiritual and emotional blessings that are sure to follow.

FOOD FOR THOUGHT
YOUR DIET REFLECTS YOUR VALUES

If you place a high value on the body God has given you, then place high importance on the foods you use to fuel it.

MORE FROM GOD'S WORD

The LORD is my strength and my song; he has become my victory. He is my God, and I will praise him.

Exodus 15:2 NLT

Be careful not to forget the Lord.

Deuteronomy 6:12 HCSB

It is good to give thanks to the Lord, and to sing praises to Your name, O Most High; to declare Your lovingkindness in the morning, and Your faithfulness every night.

Psalm 92:1-2 NKJV

Love the Lord your God with all your heart, with all your soul, and with all your strength.

Deuteronomy 6:5 HCSB

The Devil said to Him, "I will give You their splendor and all this authority, because it has been given over to me, and I can give it to anyone I want. If You, then, will worship me, all will be Yours." And Jesus answered him, "It is written: You shall worship the Lord your God, and Him alone you shall serve."

Luke 4:6-8 HCSB

MORE THOUGHTS ABOUT
PUTTING GOD FIRST

Make God's will the focus of your life day by day. If you seek to please Him and Him alone, you'll find yourself satisfied with life.

Kay Arthur

Jesus Christ is the first and last, author and finisher, beginning and end, alpha and omega, and by Him all other things hold together. He must be first or nothing. God never comes next!

Vance Havner

Do not be afraid, then, that if you trust, or tell others to trust, the matter will end there. Trust is only the beginning and the continual foundation. When we trust Him, the Lord works, and His work is the important part of the whole matter.

Hannah Whitall Smith

Our body is a portable sanctuary through which we are daily experiencing the presence of God.

Richard Foster

PERFECTION IS IMPOSSIBLE

You don't have to be perfect to be wonderful. The difference between perfectionism and realistic expectations is the difference between a life of frustration and a life of contentment. Only one earthly being ever lived life to perfection, and He was the Son of God. The rest of us have fallen short of God's standard and need to be accepting of our own limitations as well as the limitations of others.

If you find yourself frustrated by the unrealistic demands of others (or by unrealistic pressures of the self-imposed variety), it's time to ask yourself who you're trying to impress, and why. Your first responsibility is to the Heavenly Father who created you and to the Son who saved you. Then, you bear a powerful responsibility to be true to yourself. And of course you owe debts of gratitude to friends and family members. But, when it comes to meeting society's unrealistic expectations, forget it! Those expectations aren't just unrealistic; they're detrimental to your spiritual health.

So, if you're a woman who has become discouraged with your inability to be perfectly fit, remember that when you accepted Christ as your Savior, God accepted you for all eternity. Now, it's your turn to accept yourself. When you do, you'll feel a tremendous weight being lifted from your shoulders. After all, pleasing God is simply a matter of obeying His commandments and accepting His Son. But as for pleasing everybody else? That's impossible . . . so why even try?

WORKING IT OUT
IT'S POSSIBLE TO GET FIT AND STAY FIT

Would you like to continue your journey toward improved fitness? Then start with the firm conviction that God wants the very same thing. And then have faith that when you and God work together, anything is possible!

CELEBRATING LIFE

Today is a non-renewable resource—once it's gone, it's gone forever. Our responsibility, as thoughtful believers, is to use this day in the service of God's will and in the service of His people. When we do so, we enrich our own lives and the lives of those whom we love.

God has richly blessed us, and He wants you to rejoice in His gifts. That's why this day—and each day that follows—should be a time of prayer and celebration as we consider the Good News of God's free gift: salvation through Jesus Christ.

Oswald Chambers correctly observed, "Joy is the great note all throughout the Bible." E. Stanley Jones echoed that thought when he wrote "Christ and joy go together." But, even the most dedicated Christians can, on occasion, forget to celebrate each day for what it is: a priceless gift from God.

What do you expect from the day ahead? Are you expecting God to do wonderful things, or are you living beneath a cloud of apprehension and doubt? The familiar words of Psalm 118:24 remind us of a profound yet simple truth: "This is the day which the LORD hath made" (KJV). Our duty, as believers, is to rejoice in God's marvelous creation.

Today, celebrate the life that God has given you. Today, put a smile on your face, kind words on your lips, and a song in your heart. Be generous with your praise and free with your encouragement. And then, when you have celebrated life to the fullest, invite your friends to do likewise. After all, this is God's day, and He has given us clear instructions for its use. We are commanded to rejoice and be glad. So, with no further ado, let the celebration begin...

MORE FROM GOD'S WORD
ABOUT JOY

Rejoice in the Lord always. I will say it again: Rejoice!

Philippians 4:4 HCSB

You will show me the way of life, granting me the joy of your presence and the pleasures of living with you forever.

Psalm 16:11 NLT

David and the whole house of Israel were celebrating before the Lord.

2 Samuel 6:5 HCSB

Their sorrow was turned into rejoicing and their mourning into a holiday. They were to be days of feasting, rejoicing, and of sending gifts to one another and the poor.

Esther 9:22 HCSB

STRENGTHENING YOUR FAITH
HIS RIGHTFUL PLACE

You must guard your heart by putting God in His rightful place—first place.

NOTES TO YOURSELF

Are you putting God first in every aspect of your life? In the space below, describe how you believe God wants you to treat your body.

_____

_____

_____

_____

_____

_____

_____

_____

_____

_____

_____

_____

_____

_____

_____

_____

_____